The Essential
Guide to Rhetoric

The Essential Guide to Rhetoric

William M. Keith
University of Wisconsin, Milwaukee

Christian O. Lundberg
University of North Carolina, Chapel Hill

BEDFORD / ST. MARTIN'S

Boston ◆ New York

Manufactured in the United States of America.

1 0 9 8 7
f e d c b a

For information, write: Bedford/St. Martin's, 75 Arlington Street, Boston, MA 02116 (617-399-4000)

ISBN-10: 0-312-47239-0
ISBN-13: 978-0-312-47239-9

Acknowledgments
"rhetoric" from *The American Heritage Dictionary of the English Language,* Fourth Edition. Copyright © 2006 by Houghton Mifflin Company. Reproduced by permission from *The American Heritage Dictionary of the English Language,* Fourth Edition.

PREFACE

The Essential Guide to Rhetoric is a versatile supplement for students who need a brief, topical introduction to the key concepts of rhetoric. In addition to discussions of history, speech situations, and tropes, the text also connects rhetorical theory to contemporary issues in students' lives: public speaking, online communication, and engagement in political discourse.

WHY AN *ESSENTIAL GUIDE TO RHETORIC*?

We believe that gaining an understanding of rhetorical theory and its practical applications is a critical component to effective and competent communication. But not everyone has the opportunity to study rhetoric in detail, particularly at the undergraduate level where courses such as public speaking and the introductory communication survey tend to be the first requirement. A very basic knowledge of rhetorical concepts can enrich students' experience in these and other courses, but survey textbooks tend to offer minimal coverage at this level. Many instructors crave more depth but do not need a full-blown rhetoric survey—they just supplement with bits and pieces.

With this in mind, we saw a need for a handy booklet that explains the basics of persuasion in a brief and accessible way. We wrote *The Essential Guide to Rhetoric* to cover classic and modern rhetorical theory in ways that would intrigue today's students and satisfy instructors' teaching needs. This guide helps students identify, understand, and employ the core tenets of rhetoric through a solid foundation in theory balanced by engaging language and current examples. Our ultimate desire is to provide the necessary groundwork while sparking an interest in students to learn more and employ this knowledge in their lives.

STRUCTURE AND COVERAGE

To help guide readers through the text, *The Essential Guide to Rhetoric* is split into two parts: Part I, "Rhetoric in Theory," which provides a succinct overview of the foundations of rhetoric, and Part II, "Rhetoric in Action," which shows how the rhetorical concepts come to life. Topic coverage includes:

- A clear definition of rhetoric and its components (Chapter 1).
- A brief discussion of the development of rhetoric from ancient Greece to today (Chapter 1).
- A thorough explanation of the audience's role in rhetoric, including how traditional audiences evolved to publics, strategies for adapting to audiences, the role of language in persuasion, and the importance of ethics (Chapter 2).
- An overview of classical concepts—speech types, speech purposes, rhetorical situations—juxtaposed with more contemporary theories of rhetorical situations from Lloyd Bitzer and Michael Calvin McGee (Chapter 3).
- An explanation of argument from the basics of proofs (logos, ethos, pathos) and forms of argument to stock issues, topoi, and fallacies (Chapter 4).
- Coverage of how to understand the organization of a speech: organizational patterns, parts of a speech, and a sample speech (Chapter 5).
- A guide to using style in persuasive speech: figures and tropes (Chapter 6).
- How rhetoric applies to our contemporary lives: public speaking, online communication, and politics (Chapter 7).

By moving students from rhetorical concept to action, the text is an accessible first step for anyone desiring a deeper grasp of the rhetorical tradition.

This booklet is available either as a stand-alone text or packaged with *A Speaker's Guidebook, A Pocket Guide to Public Speaking,* and a number of other Bedford/St. Martin's communication titles—including the booklets *The Essential Guide to Group Communication* and *The Essential Guide to Interpersonal Communication.* For more information on these or other Bedford/St. Martin's communication texts, please visit www.bedfordstmartins.com.

We are grateful to everyone at Bedford/St. Martin's who supported this project through its many stages: Joan Feinberg, Denise Wydra, Erika Gutierrez, Erica Appel, and Casey Carroll. We also collaborated with developmental editors Noel Hohnstine and Simon Glick, and the helpful production team: Shuli Traub, Ryan Sullivan, and Dennis J. Conroy.

William M. Keith
Christian O. Lundberg

CONTENTS

PART I
Rhetoric in Theory

The Rhetorical Tradition **1**

Imagine a presidential candidate arguing in a televised debate for sweeping domestic reform; fighting an uphill battle, the candidate carefully chooses every word to reflect themes discovered by months of polling. A family watching the debate changes the channel, flipping from station to station, and lands on a commercial for a luxury car. The commercial features images of a highly manicured couple sitting in an even more highly manicured leather interior. The message is clear: buying this car signals success and status to one's friends and neighbors. Earlier that day, a defense attorney argued passionately in front of a jury for a client who was probably guilty. Daydreaming, the client looked at the flag in the courtroom and nostalgically remembered when elementary school classes opened with the pledge of allegiance.

What connects these seemingly unrelated events? In each instance, whether through media, direct address, memory, or otherwise, people are being persuaded to act, think, and do certain things through language or symbols. And that process, perhaps, at least in part, is what makes up the study of rhetoric.

DEFINING RHETORIC

What exactly is rhetoric? One of the persistent problems in defining and thinking about rhetoric is that people use the term in so many different ways. Consider this definition from *The American Heritage Dictionary*:

> Rhetoric, n.: **1a.** The art or study of using language effectively and persuasively. **b.** A treatise or book discussing this art. **2.** Skill in using language effectively and persuasively. **3a.** A style of speaking or writing, especially the language of a particular subject: *fiery political rhetoric.* **b.** Language that is elaborate, pretentious, insincere, or intellectually vacuous: *His offers of compromise were mere rhetoric.* **4.** Verbal communication; discourse. [1]

The core idea behind each part of this definition is that rhetoric has something to do with the relationship between language and persuasion. You can see many examples of these variations of rhetoric if you look around a bit. Tune in to CNN or Fox News, and you will hear political pundits exchanging accusations that their opponents' statements or promises are "mere" rhetoric — that they are insincere or intellectually empty. In a public speaking class, you may learn that rhetoric is essentially about style, or the ability to present yourself and your ideas persuasively. In a communication studies journal, you may find rhetoricians (people who formally study rhetoric) using the term *rhetoric* to label the word choices, styles, and argument strategies in a speech, movie, Web site, or book. If you pick up a text by a philosopher who studies language, you may find a definition claiming that all language is "rhetorical"; that is, far from being simply about rules or syntax, language is always connected to a context, and people use language to figure out meaning within that context. Ironically, this definition is the opposite of the political talk show meaning of rhetoric: for the pundit attacking an opponent, rhetoric is false speech that doesn't match reality; but for some philosophers and linguists, rhetoric *is* reality.

Rhetoric may be confusing at first because it can refer to all these things: empty words, a style of speaking, specific speeches or texts, a skill or knack, even language in general. But don't feel overwhelmed. In this *Essential Guide to Rhetoric*, we will sort out the various definitions and give you the tools to think about them. To begin, let's look at the two concepts most commonly associated with rhetoric: discourse and persuasion. A **discourse** can be any speech, written or spoken, as well as the exchange of symbols or meanings in any context: books, newspapers, pictures, movies, Web sites, music, and so on. **Persuasion** occurs when someone convinces you of something; it encompasses the dramatic experience of being moved to rage, tears, or action by a speech, as well as more subtle processes such as being influenced by advertising or political ideology. Rhetoric ties these two concepts together. In this book, we will define **rhetoric** as *the study of producing discourses and interpreting how, when, and why discourses are persuasive.* In other words, rhetoric is about how discourses get things done in our social world. Whether you study rhetoric only for its influence on speech or as a broad system of symbols and persuasion, this guide will explain the various branches of rhetoric and provide a base of knowledge for your particular understanding of the term.

RHETORIC IN PRACTICE

What does it mean that rhetoric is about getting things done in our social world? Think of it this way: there are a number of things you can do by yourself. You can choose to get up from where you're sitting, put this book down, yell, scream, or jump up and down. But more complex tasks require the cooperation of other people. For example, if you want to borrow notes for a missed class, get a political candidate elected, or convince people that they should do something about global warming, you need varying degrees of cooperation. Of course, you could achieve these goals by stealing notes for the class, physically forcing people to vote, or bribing lawmakers, but such approaches are risky, complicated, and illegal. So how can you get things done without using these sorts of tactics?

More often than not, you can do so by getting other people to help you, usually by persuading them to take up your preferred course of action or point of view. Everything you do with other people involves their explicit or implicit cooperation, and cooperation requires an element of persuasion. In other words, political and social action at every level, from your family and closest friends to national and international politics, requires some form of cooperation and persuasion. Persuasion can be active (your attempts to convince a professor to change a grade) or passive (advertising's attempts to influence consumers to buy a product by featuring sexy images or promises of a better lifestyle). Persuasion might also target a specific goal such as "Vote for Proposition 56" or something more abstract like cultivating patriotism. Whether active or passive; specific or general; in the political, social, intellectual, or other spheres; persuasion is the key to coordinated action. Persuasion is the glue that holds people to a common purpose and therefore facilitates collective action.

THE ORIGINS OF RHETORIC

Of course, people were using words and symbols to influence one another long before the idea of rhetoric was invented. Yet at a certain point, thinkers began to wonder how this process happened and how they could talk about it more effectively. Although scholars don't know exactly where or how this came about, they do know that the term *rhetoric* originated in Athens, Greece, sometime around the fifth century BCE.

RHETORIC IN ANCIENT GREECE

Athens in the fifth century BCE was a bustling metropolis, and people from all over the Mediterranean area were immigrating there. The Greek city-state was experimenting with a new form of government — democracy, or rule by the *demos,* the "people." (At that time, people's political and cultural identity was tied to the city area in which they lived.) Today, we are used to the idea of democracy, but a new democracy requires many new social practices — such as how to resolve disputes without turning to an authority like a king, how to make laws by common consent, and how to decide which direction society should take. The citizens of Athens formed institutions to direct these processes: a senate, jury trials, and forums for public discussion. But people needed to learn how to navigate these new institutions. With no mass media, no printing presses, and very few written texts, the primary vehicle of discussion and information distribution was speech. The Athenians needed a strategy for effectively talking to other people in juries, in forums, and in the senate.

In the fifth century BCE, a group of wandering Sicilians, who later became known as Sophists, started to teach Athenians how to speak persuasively with the goal of navigating the courts and senate. The name *Sophists* indicated that these speech teachers claimed to be purveyors of wisdom (*sophia* is Greek for "wisdom" and the root term for *philosophy,* or "love of wisdom"), and *Sophists* came to be the common term for someone who sold wisdom for money.

Though it is not clear how or why this group became interested in teaching persuasive speech, we do know that as Athenian citizens relied more and more on public speech to deal with their new political processes, the market for sophistic training increased. Sophists were perhaps the earliest consultants: they offered training in winning legal cases, speaking persuasively in the forum, and arguing in public.

Facility in speaking may have made an Athenian citizen more effective in winning over juries, and it may have been a prerequisite to democracy, but it also made people nervous. Why? Some feared that teaching people to be more persuasive meant that falsehood would prevail over truth—that highly trained speakers would defeat truthful opponents who were not as persuasive. Plato, a fifth-century Athenian philosopher, claimed that rhetoric was a disconnected set of techniques without a central ethical concern or philosophical system. For Plato, rhetoric was dangerous because it did not have the rigor of a scientific enterprise or the critical quality of a philosophical endeavor; rather, it was a group of random techniques that helped those in the wrong win support for their cause.

However, Aristotle (384–322 BCE), a student of Plato and one whom many scholars credit with being the first theorist of rhetoric, disagreed that persuasive technique was only a way of making "the weaker case the stronger." Instead, Aristotle saw rhetoric as a **techne**—an art or technique—of human speech that could be both a coherent system for classifying, studying, and interpreting speeches and a skill for public dialogue. Aristotle argued three basic points:

- *Rhetoric can be treated as a coherent area of inquiry.* Rhetoric is not simply a collection of techniques for slick speech; it also has a logic and a purpose as the "faculty of observing the available means of persuasion in any given situation."[2] In other words, by taking into account the specific qualities of an audience, a setting, and an occasion, an orator (or speaker) can figure out exactly what would be persuasive in that context.

- *Rhetoric and logic are necessary counterparts.* Rhetoric and logic (Aristotle and Plato called logic *dialectic*) are not opposites but mutually complementary and necessary counterparts: logic requires persuasion, and persuasion requires logic.

- *The form and function of speeches are shaped by the possible speech goals.* The logic and coherence of speeches are determined by their goals. To clarify this point, Aristotle classified different kinds of speech by their purposes: **forensic** (for use at a trial), **epideictic** (for use at a funeral), and **deliberative** (for use in the senate). He choose these types of speeches as the basis for his classification system because they have different goals and relationships to time and action, not because they are the only possible kinds of speeches. Let's take a closer look at the functions of each type of speech in the following table:

ARISTOTLE'S TYPES OF SPEECHES

Type of Speech	Purpose	Example
Forensic		
From the Greek *dikanikos*, meaning "judicial" or "skilled at law": a speech that is given in a public forum, such as in front of an Athenian jury.	*Justice:* To determine what happened in the past, such as arguing for guilt or innocence.	A lawyer's closing statement.
Epideictic		
From the Greek *epideixis*, meaning "to shine" or "to show forth": a speech that displays the qualities of something.	*Honor:* To say how people should feel in the present, and to assign praise or blame.	A eulogy at a funeral.
Deliberative		
From the term *sumbou-leutikos*, meaning "to weigh" or "to consider": a speech that argues for a course of action.	*Utility:* To make a case for what people should or should not do in the future, such as avoiding harmful things and doing good.	A debate over the passage of a law.

Aristotle also created a classification system for rhetorical **proofs**, the ways of making speech persuasive. He divided proofs into three categories: *logos* (logic), *ethos* (credibility of the speaker), and *pathos* (emotional appeal). All three elements play a role in persuasion—a good persuasive speech needs to be attentive to the audience by applying logic, demonstrating the speaker's credibility, and appealing to the audience's emotions. (For more on proofs, see Chapter 4.)

Whether or not one agrees with Aristotle's system, which may be too simplistic for the variety of speeches and speech acts that we see today, it definitely marked rhetoric as an important and systematic area of scholarly study and a central part of human political and social life. Aristotle demonstrated the possibilities for becoming more persuasive and figuring out what motivates people to action.

RHETORIC ACROSS THE AGES

Even though the Athenians were the first to fully theorize rhetoric, they were not the last to think about issues of speech, symbols, and persuasion. In the course of this text, we'll mostly refer to the modern-day study and uses of rhetoric while occasionally referencing other parts of rhetoric's history. But first, let's consider how rhetoric evolved from ancient Greece to the present day.

Throughout the history of the Western world, many scholars, philosophers, and other intellectuals have returned to rhetoric. The following is a brief but by no means complete list of important rhetorical periods and figures:

- *1st century BCE.* Cicero, a Roman orator, philosopher, and statesman, wrote extensively on rhetoric and specifically on oratory. (Cicero defined three kinds of speeches; see Chapter 3.) Quintilian, another Roman, also did work on rhetoric, concentrating on the idea of trope, which would become significant later. Basically, trope encompasses the different ways that a speaker can play with language—by using metaphors, vivid images, repetition, and so on (see Chapter 6).

- *4th century CE.* Augustine of Hippo, a theologian and saint of the Catholic Church, picked up where the Greeks and Romans left off, arguing that philosophy and theology required rhetoric as a way of making truth intelligible to people who were not theologians or philosophers.

- *5th century CE to the 15th century (approximately).* By the Middle Ages, rhetoric made up one-third of the required subjects in the humanistic arts. During that time, students in any respectable curriculum were required to learn Grammar, Logic, and Rhetoric.

- *14th century CE to the 17th century (approximately).* During the Renaissance, rhetoric flowered and rhetoricians turned to the arts of speech and letter writing as part of a new commitment to eloquence in the courts, palaces, and salons of kings and other leaders. Erasmus and Ramus were Renaissance humanists who expanded the rhetorical tradition.

- *17th and 18th centuries.* Thinkers such as Thomas Hobbes, John Locke, Jean-Jacques Rousseau, Giambattista Vico, and Hugh Blair became increasingly interested in the relationship among rhetoric, politics, human knowledge, and human nature.

Even when people were not explicitly studying rhetoric, rhetorical processes were at work every time people spoke, wrote, or acted to persuade others. This rich history of academic theorization and everyday rhetorical practice became the basis for the contemporary discipline of rhetoric.

RHETORIC TODAY

Aristotle's book *Rhetoric* has been studied for more than twenty-five hundred years. Though modern society does not have public forums for resolving disputes in the same way Athenians did, the rhetorical concepts arising out of this tradition can help us think about our own times, challenges, and condition. Through the lens of rhetoric, we can gain important insights about the contemporary world in three important areas: identity and power, visual and material symbols, and the public and democracy.

IDENTITY AND POWER

Let's start by looking at the concepts of identity and power. What do we mean by identity? Say you are filling out a Facebook or MySpace profile. What kinds of questions do such Web sites ask, or what information might you offer to define who you are? You might include biographical information like your age and hometown, but you also might identify your sex, sexual orientation, race, nationality, religion, and so on. Your identity is the set of labels, patterns of behavior, and ways of representing yourself that make up your public persona. What does this have to do with power? Well, political power and social status are linked to the identity categories with which you affiliate—not just in terms of institutional representation (whether there are people who think, sound, and look like you in political office), but also in terms of how you move through the social world and are treated by others.

Because rhetoric concerns the way that symbols and discourses are persuasive—how they influence our thoughts, habits, and actions—we can approach the question of identity by asking: How are specific discourses of identity persuasive? How do they influence public life? How do discourses of discrimination become widely accepted—that is, persuasive? How do people draw on their discourse of identity to cope with daily existence? Rhetoric helps us understand how certain identities are persuasive and why certain identity practices and labels seem to facilitate political power. Thus, even though the beginnings of rhetoric focused on the narrow context of persuasive public speech, rhetoric today can serve more broadly to help us think about issues of identity and power.

VISUAL AND MATERIAL SYMBOLS

Rhetoric can help us explore the visual and material world because, at its root, it is about discourses and symbols. We can gain a better understanding of modern life by exploring how visual symbols (things that we see) and material symbols (things that we physically interact with, like statues and monuments) persuade us to act, think, or believe in certain ways. Rhetoric can apply to a wide range of objects of study beyond speech; in fact, rhetoricians have studied the persuasive qualities of graphic design, advertisements, movies, Web sites, museums, monuments, graffiti, radio hosts, television, and so on. Rhetoric, as a technique, allows us to put each object into a critical (or interpretive) framework and ask the following questions: Who is looking at these objects? Where, when, and why are they looking at them? What political and social statements do the objects make? How do people react to them? Are the objects persuasive (do they do what they were intended to do)? The move to study visual and material symbols is an important branch of the rhetorical tradition, enabling rhetoricians to apply the basic rhetorical framework (audience, discourse, point of origin) to the visual and material elements (especially in mass media) that affect our lives the most.

THE PUBLIC AND DEMOCRACY

If Athens was a young democracy that needed rhetoric to help its citizens with the public speech required by new social institutions, what does today's much older and more complicated democracy need from rhetoric? Today, rhetoric can be a way of exploring the relationship between communication and democracy in modern America. It can examine the ways that political messages (like campaign commercials), representations, and habits are constructed and repeated, and the reasons why such elements are persuasive for particular groups of people or voters.

The questions of identity and power, visual and material elements, and the public and democracy represent some of the possibilities for rhetoric as a modern interpretive technique. Thus, as we work through the rest of this guide, we will refer both to the ancient problem of rhetoric and to some of its more contemporary applications.

Rhetoric and the Audience 2

The audience is a crucial element in rhetorical study. If you want to understand how and why a symbol, speech, or message is persuasive, you cannot simply focus on the speaker or on what he or she says; you also need to focus on the people to whom the symbol, speech, or message is directed—the **audience**.

To be successfully persuasive, you need to figure out exactly whom you want to persuade and what would convince them. The idea of the audience (or its modern equivalent, the public) includes the individuals with interests and biases who make up the audience, the situation that the audience finds itself in, and the challenge of proper timing. To persuade an audience, a speaker needs to say the right thing to the right people in the right situation, at the right time, and with the right ethical conditions.

Cumulatively, these factors influence the ways that a speaker relates to an audience. In doing so, they help rhetoricians to figure out both how to "read" audiences and why some arguments are persuasive and others aren't. Thus, thinking about audience may be the most important rhetorical skill.

THE AUDIENCE'S ROLE

All rhetoric is a form of communication, but not all communication is rhetoric. The audience is specific to rhetorical communication and is a key factor in distinguishing the two. How? Let's start by looking at the four-element process all communication follows:

- First, there is a **message**, or the content that someone or something seeks to convey.
- Second, someone or something sends a message. This is the **sender**. Depending on the area of communication being studied, the sender may be a speaker (in public speaking), an institution (in organizational communication), a cable broadcaster (in mass communication), or any number of other points of origin.
- Third, communication requires a **receiver**—someone, something, or some group (such as an audience) that receives the message.
- Fourth, there is the **medium** (plural, **media**), the means of transmitting information between sender and receiver. The medium may be a speech, a radio wave, a film, a book, an e-mail, and so on.

In a conversation, perhaps the most basic form of communication, the person who is speaking is the sender, the one who is listening is the receiver, and the speaker's voice is the medium, which carries the message. Some communication can be relatively automatic. For example, think about the communication that occurs when your hard drive sends data to your computer screen: there is a sender (the hard drive), a receiver (the screen), a medium (binary code sent through the processor to the screen, carried by electrical current), and a message (everything that appears on the screen). You might even consider biological processes as a kind of communication: when you're hungry, your empty stomach (the sender) sends a signal to your brain (receiver) through your nervous system (medium) that your brain decodes as hunger (message).

But rhetorical communication is not automatic like these exchanges. Where does rhetoric fit in the communication process? Consider how the receiver, or audience, functions in rhetoric. The presence of an audience allows rhetorical communication to be about more than the message or the speaker; its presence adds a key role for the way those elements are perceived. In rhetorical communication, the interaction is between two self-aware agents. Audiences have their own opinions and predispositions; therefore, instead of automatically compelling a particular response, successful rhetoric depends on persuasion — getting the audience to agree with the speaker. As a result, rhetoric always has two characteristics that make it distinct from communication:

- *Rhetoric is contingent.* Rhetorical communication is always **contingent**: the outcome of a rhetorical act depends on audience reaction. Since every audience is unique and has its own predispositions, the audience might be persuaded, but it might also be bored by or become angry at the speaker.
- *Rhetoric is strategic.* Because rhetoric is tied to the contingencies of the audience, it is **strategic**: the speaker must figure out how to deliver the message in a way that garners a positive audience reaction.

CLASSICAL STRATEGIES FOR THINKING ABOUT AUDIENCES

Audiences have always played a crucial role in rhetorical theory and criticism. Yet as rhetoric evolved from ancient Greece to the modern world of mass media, the ways that rhetoricians view audiences have also changed. Let's take a closer look at some of the ways that rhetoricians have thought about approaching audiences in order to figure out how to persuade them.

"READING" AN AUDIENCE

One of the oldest existing documents on the power of rhetoric is a speech by the Sophist Gorgias called "The Encomium for Helen."[1] (As discussed in Chapter 1, a Sophist is a person who taught ancient Greeks how to be persuasive; an encomium is a speech that commemorates a person or thing.) This encomium portrays audiences as virtually helpless against the power of well-crafted, persuasive words.

In his speech, Gorgias attempts to exonerate Helen of Troy from starting the Trojan War. (Helen ran off with Paris, a prince of Troy. Her husband, the king of Sparta, started a war to get her back.) Gorgias argues that Helen could not help herself if she was won over by the power of Paris's words, because any audience at any time can be persuaded of anything if they are provided a sufficiently good speech.

But Aristotle, who in part responds to such a view of audiences, argues that audiences are not helpless dupes. Being well aware of the problems presented by the great variety of audiences, he claims that every instance with a speaker represents a fundamentally different situation. He thus recognizes (contradicting Gorgias) that rhetoric is not a universal magic that sways audiences, but a strategic art that seeks the best way of figuring out what to say to an audience in a given situation. This task requires as much of a facility for "reading" an audience as for composing speeches. Contemporary rhetoricians — such as Black, Bitzer, and McGee (whom we discuss later) — extend Aristotle's understanding of rhetoric by theorizing that audiences and speech situations are unruly, and that what works for one audience under certain circumstances may not work for another audience under the same circumstances — or even the same audience under different circumstances. (For more on this topic, see Chapter 3.)

TIMING

Finding the right combination of audience, circumstance, and message is not the only challenge that a rhetorician faces in persuading an audience. There is also the issue of timing. The Greeks used the term *kairos* to describe the right time to say something. This term had a nonrhetorical origin; it originally meant a narrow slit in a wall through which a soldier would shoot an arrow. If the target was moving and the soldier only had a very narrow gap, the timing of the shot was crucial. In rhetoric, **kairos** means that there is an exactly right time to deliver a message if the audience is to be persuaded. For example, a savvy teenager wouldn't ask her parents for extra spending money right after getting a bad report card or if her family is in financial trouble; likewise, the great speeches of the civil rights movement might not have been as well received if they had been given a hundred years earlier.

ARE AUDIENCES MADE OR FOUND?

The idea that persuasion is contingent upon the audience's characteristics assumes that the audience possesses defining characteristics before the speaker addresses it. However, it's also possible for the speaker to play a role in composing, or evoking, the audience in a persuasive situation.

Consider the idea of persona, or the roles and images that we imagine for ourselves and others. The idea of persona comes from the Greek term *prosopon*, which means "person" but also means "mask," like the mask that someone might wear in a play. For example, while reading a gritty adventure novel full of high action and tough talk, you may develop a mental image of the author as a tanned, leather-skinned, scarred, and muscular man of action sitting at a computer terminal chewing on a cigar butt. Of course, the author may be a pale, frail, elderly woman, but the point is that the author projects an image. This is the first persona — or, in the terms of classical rhetoric, the ethos of the author or speaker.

Does the audience have a persona? Modern rhetorician Edwin Black (1929–2007) thought so; he called it the **second persona**.[2] This perspective views the audience as not existing, so to speak, independent of the speaker, but as created in response to the speaker. In other words, a particular kind of argument from a speaker can *evoke*, or bring about, a particular audience. If a speaker talking about school funding makes her arguments about financial issues ("How much do schools cost?" or "How can we save money?"), she appeals to, and calls forth, an audience of consumers. This not a physically different group of people, but her arguments ask listeners to see themselves as consumers. Alternatively, another speaker might focus on educational quality and community pride, implicitly asking audience members to respond as citizens rather than as consumers.

The second persona means that the actual people making up the audience at the beginning of the speech take on another identity that the speaker convinces them to inhabit through the course of the speech itself. For example, if a speaker says, "We, as concerned citizens, must act to take care of the environment," he is not only trying to get audience members to do something about the environment but also attempting to get them to identify themselves as concerned citizens.

Consider another example: the preamble to the U.S. constitution. The effect of the second persona makes it a powerful rhetorical document. Though we don't think about it much now, there was a time when people considered themselves only British colonists or citizens of a specific state. When the colonists recognized themselves as Americans, as "we the people of the United States," the Constitution *created* a specifically American audience.

FROM AUDIENCES TO PUBLICS

So far, we have discussed an audience as a group of people gathered in the presence of a speaker and as a group of people who respond to a speaker. But in the contemporary era characterized by a saturated media environment, audiences also include a wide variety of listeners or viewers who encounter a dizzying array of messages in the mass media. Today, we are equally comfortable talking about the "audience" attending a commencement speech, the "audience" that tunes in to *The Oprah Winfrey Show* every afternoon, and the "audience" of this book. In light of this change, rhetoricians have reevaluated what it means to be an audience.

DEFINING A PUBLIC AUDIENCE

How is an audience attending a speech different from one that watches it on TV or reads it in a book? The difference is in the nature of the audience and speaker relationship—how personal or impersonal it is. **Address** is the formal term for the relationship between a speaker or sender and an audience or receiver. Imagine a continuum of all the different types of speaker and audience relationships. On one end, there is a single speaker who seeks to persuade a single person of the merits of a specific course of action—for example, buying a car or going on a date. On the opposite end is "the media" consisting of multiple "speakers" (remember, anything that seeks to persuade can be a speech) with multiple purposes whose "speech" targets multiple audiences at the same time—for example, a CNN news broadcast or a movie.

Newer, technology-driven forms of audience present a challenge for classic rhetorical vocabulary: does it still make sense to talk about audiences as we move along the continuum toward the mass media? After all, when people watch a TV show, they are not an audience in the same way that people attending a speech are: the viewers and "speakers" can't interact via TV in the same way, the diversity of TV viewers may be much greater than that of an audience listening to a speech, there is no way of "reading" the audience during the show to adapt to it, and the TV relationship is much more about consumption than interaction or dialogue. How can rhetoric treat such an audience?

One response is to talk about a special kind of audience—a **public**, or the commonality among people that is based on consumption of common texts (shared experience in society). To better understand what a public is, consider that in the modern world we are much more comfortable with strangers than our ancestors were. Imagine a premodern village where everyone knows everyone else and they rarely encounter strangers because our villagers already have relationships with most of the people they encounter. If they didn't know a person directly, they might know his family, his job, his house of worship, and so on. When the villagers did encounter strangers, they usually viewed them with suspicion.

This premodern village serves as a counterpoint to our lives today. We are surrounded by strangers all the time and are not too bothered by it. You are probably comfortable interacting with strangers in a thousand ways that you do not even notice—you buy things from them, you ask them for the time, you sit in class with them, you go to movies with them, you ride on buses and subways with them. One way of explaining why you are comfortable with strangers is that you share things with them that premodern villagers did not: you have a common national identity; you may read the same newspapers, surf the same Web sites, listen to the same music, and watch the same TV shows. You are part of the same public as strangers; in other words, you share a larger culture. These changes caused rhetoricians to reconsider not only how to define an audience but also how to deal with a public audience in rhetorical communication.

THREE WAYS OF TALKING ABOUT PUBLICS

There are many ways of understanding what a public is, most of which explain the sense of commonality with other people. Three of the most common conceptions are common goods and the public sphere, indirect effects, and address.

Common Goods and the Public Sphere

The word *public,* in everyday use, often indicates shared or *common goods*—for example, public services such as trash collection, public utilities such as water and electricity, or the upkeep on roads and bridges. *Public* also applies as a label for areas that are open and accessible to everyone, such as public parks or town squares. We can combine these two meanings—common goods and places open to all—to think about the meaning of *public* in rhetorical terms. The traditional term for this rhetorical idea is **public sphere**, a place common to all where ideas and information are exchanged. This place is anywhere people interact outside the bounds of their private lives to engage in communication with strangers or in public acts or discussions—for example, voting, attending a protest, going to a lecture, and so on. It does not have to be a physically public place.

Unlike the public sphere, the *private sphere* encompasses what happens within the bounds of one's home or among close relatives and friends. Note that the private sphere is also not limited to locations; it concerns anyone whom a person interacts with—for example, a private conversation.

Indirect Effects

Public communication can also be defined by what a person is talking about and how she talks about it. The American philosopher John Dewey (1859–1952) said that people are talking in public whenever they talk about the *indirect effects* of their actions on others.[3] Dewey contrasted the idea of a private conversation (where, for instance, you might negotiate with a friend about exchanging notes for a class) and a "public" conversation (where you and the same friend might argue about the merits of a presidential candidate). What is the difference between the two? A conversation about class notes mostly has implications for you and your friend, but a political argument has implications not only for the two of you but also for everyone else the candidate might impact. For Dewey, a conversation, argument, or speech becomes public as soon as it focuses on other people, whom the speakers may not even know, who may be affected by it.

The core difference between the public and private spheres is not where the discussion occurs or what it is talking about, but the way that it is framed. A public discussion can't just rely on personal bias ("I hate the president because he has beady eyes.") or take place in front of other people. Instead, a public argument has to be based on publicly available reasons for common concern ("I think the president's economic policy will hurt the poor.").

Address

Address is a way of saying that a speaker and an audience have a relationship whereby each understands what the other is doing. In the setting of a public speech, when a speaker addresses an audience then the audience recognizes her as the speaker.

What happens if we apply this model to the mass media (and therefore a public audience)? For example, how do you recognize that the newspaper is addressing you? One commonsense answer is to say that of course the newspaper is intended for you, since by definition the mass media produces messages for the public, and you are a part of the public. But "you are a part of the public" is the interesting part of this answer: it reveals a good bit about how we understand our relationship to other people. It is a fact of modern life that we think of ourselves as part of a larger social body that is linked by attention to common texts such as television, movies, radio, Web sites, newspapers, and the like. This understanding of common address highlights our "public" role in relation to the mass media and other consumers of mass media.

Rhetoric encompasses these three views of the public. Each view depends on people being persuaded by texts. Rhetoric studies how, why, when, and for whom texts are persuasive, and how they contribute to our understanding of the social world. It is the key to understanding how we function as a public.

ADAPTING TO AUDIENCES AND PUBLICS

The many different types of audiences that can be present in a rhetorical situation vary not only in size and classification but also in membership. Audiences may be relatively homogeneous (having similar identities and interests) or significantly diverse. Sometimes audience members share very few traits, values, or beliefs, reflecting a random set of differences. For example, some people may attend a school board meeting as consumers and some as citizens; some may care most about elementary schools, others about high schools;

some may be concerned about truancy, others about honor class offerings. Alternatively, there may be well-defined groups in the audience with specific interests, as when just two groups attend a school board meeting: those who want to raise taxes to expand educational programs, and those who don't.

It is the speaker's challenge to address audience members in all possible situations. While this may seem daunting, there are general guidelines and techniques that can help you figure out how to best appeal to different audiences.

WHAT IS ADAPTATION?

Given that audiences are such a complex and slippery beast—sometimes unified, sometimes fragmented, and changing across time—the difficulty in persuading a specific audience or public is in figuring out what strategies to employ for each one in specific situations. The principle that guides the use of rhetorical techniques to deal with audiences has many names: appropriateness, decorum, and **adaptation**. Generally speaking, this means that speakers try to connect their audiences or public to what they are saying by choosing arguments whose premises, reasons, examples, and figures of speech relate to audience members' knowledge and experience.

Speakers typically have a goal when they approach an audience, and they accomplish that goal by using language and communication appropriately and fitting their speech to the unique qualities of the audience. In a sense, in any situation there is a right and a wrong thing to say, but can we ever *know* the right thing to say—at a party, in a speech, for a wedding toast, in a eulogy?

A number of factors influence the makeup and dispositions of any given audience and, therefore, determine what will be appropriate to say:

- *Situation:* What motivates the audience to listen to the speaker? What outcomes do they want or expect?
- *Context:* What is the broader context of the speaking situation?
- *Demographics:* What are the characteristics of the audience in terms of age, gender, race, religion, ethnic background, political affiliation, and socioeconomic status?
- *Ideology:* What beliefs, worldviews, and emotional investments does the audience bring to the situation?
- *Homogeneity/Heterogeneity:* How similar/dissimilar are most members of the audience?
- *Occasion:* What expectations are there for the speech, given the occasion? (For example, a eulogy and a political debate generate different expectations.)
- *Need:* What reason for speaking is the speaker adapting to? (This might include the public recognition of a problem.)
- *Genre:* What is the genre, or type of speech (eulogy, toast, apology, etc.)?

HOW TO ADAPT

The preceding list identifies factors that speakers can adapt to. Now let's consider some possible ways a speaker can adapt. For example, if an audience has significantly mixed viewpoints, there are two ways to adapt. First, the speaker can find a common element among the differences and, on that basis, appeal to all members as a single audience. The disadvantage of this strategy is that the common element will be fairly abstract, making it hard to provide well-adapted arguments. Second, the speaker can acknowledge each audience segment, finding arguments and ideas that suit each group. The disadvantage of this strategy is that each group will hear the appeals to the others, which may make the speaker seem manipulative and may create problems if all the appeals are not consistent. Moreover, the choice of strategy depends on the situation, so it is impossible to devise a foolproof guideline; as speakers gain experience, they generally develop a knack for "reading" the differences in situations as a guide for choosing a strategy.

A common misconception about adaptation is that it involves pandering, or just telling the audience what it wants to hear. Pandering would lead to ethical problems if what people want to hear is not true or not what the speaker believes, but it leads to practical problems as well. First, if a speaker commits himself to something he doesn't believe or can't defend, this can become problematic later — just ask all the politicians who've made promises they can't keep. Second, and more important, a speaker's goal is to persuade an audience because he believes he has something important to say, so pandering or changing his view to accommodate the audience's thinking would be self-defeating. The paradox is that the speaker has to adapt to the audience to disagree with and persuade them, so sharp disagreement is consistent with good adaptation and appropriateness to ultimately get everyone to agree.

Audiences are complex; they are made up of different people with different beliefs, values, and life experiences. The speaker wants something from the audience: their attention, their patience, their openness, a change of mind, a change of action. Indeed, the speaker's effort is not just an outlet for her own thoughts; it is, in an important sense, an effort made *on behalf of* the audience. So the speaker needs to know something about her audience beforehand to adapt the topic and presentation.

THE ROLE OF LANGUAGE

Language is a complex and flexible means of making ourselves understood, and it is fundamental to all social relations and action. Although rhetoric usually focuses on the strategic choices made in public speeches, we should keep in mind that rhetorical processes are at work anytime we employ language, and a speaker must factor them in when appealing to an audience. These processes entail two main considerations: how to choose language, and the power of language.

CHOOSING RHETORICAL LANGUAGE

As we mentioned earlier, speaking to an audience involves contingency; that is, it is dependent on audience reactions. This occurs because any of the speaker's words or sentences can be taken in a number of ways. Speakers therefore must choose their rhetorical language carefully, so the audience correctly infers their intentions. How can we move from straightforward to rhetorically effective language? Here are some elements to consider when engaging in rhetorical communication:

- *Word meaning.* When we think about how language communicates meaning, we often start by considering what words mean. For example, the word *apple* refers to a kind of fruit. But word usage can extend beyond the traditional definition. An apple can also refer to a type of thing ("The apple is one of the healthiest foods.") or function as a symbol (as in the biblical story of the garden of Eden, or in American folk tales about Johnny Appleseed). The word *apple* can also serve as a metaphor ("You are the apple of my eye.").

- *Multiple meanings.* When words have multiple meanings, this is known as **polysemy** (*poly* means "many," and *semy* implies "meaning"). For example, the word *crane* can mean either a type of bird or a type of heavy machinery. The word *bank* can mean either a place to put your money or, when used with the word *on,* the action of depending or relying on something: "You can bank on it."

- *Ambiguous meanings.* When grammar is ambiguous, this is known as **amphiboly**. Consider the sentence "Visiting relatives can be boring." It could mean either that you don't like to visit your relatives, or that you don't enjoy it when they visit you.

The complexity of language can be both a benefit and a danger to speakers. It's a benefit because it offers many ways to get a point across and many options for expression to suit a given audience and purpose. The danger is the risk of using vague or inaccurate terminology. Thus, it is important to choose language carefully and use it appropriately.

THE POWER OF LANGUAGE

Language has the power to shape our thoughts and arguments. We usually think of ourselves as "speaking the language," as controlling its meanings, but that's not always the case. Sometimes the language controls us. Think about tennis or baseball. When we play the game, we make decisions that guide our performance, but we don't think too much about the decisions we *can't* make, the options that are eliminated by the rules of the game. Hitting within the lines is taken for granted in tennis; we're not playing tennis if we don't abide by that rule.

Language doesn't have rules in the same way that a tennis game does. Of course, there are rules for spelling and grammar, and conventions for writing (writing styles like Chicago or APA), but these can change over time: new words are added to the dictionary, and new grammatical conventions replace the old. Instead of saying that language has rules, we can say that it has structure, and our ability to say or mean whatever we want may be constrained by the resources of the language we speak. As the Austrian philosopher Ludwig Wittgenstein (1889–1951) said, "The limit of my language is the limit of my world."[4]

For example, until recently *he* and *him* functioned as neuter pronouns in English ("If anyone wants a sandwich, he should go ahead and make one."). In a sense, this reflected the idea that a person, neutrally considered, was a man. If you learned to write and speak English this way, you were indirectly communicating the idea that a person = a man. Or consider the colors black and white. Typically, dark colors suggest things that are bad ("a black mark on your record," "he's in a black mood," etc.). In contrast, things that are white, light, or bright signify goodness and prosperity. We all use these metaphors without thinking, even though they also apply in the way we talk about race, in terms of "whites" and "blacks." Since these are not very accurate words in terms of skin color and they are historically related to repugnant theories about good and bad races, every time we associate villains and evil with darkness and blackness we connect ourselves, willing or not, to a whole tradition of racial theory.

Any rhetorical usage of language is necessarily tied to an audience that attempts to interpret and understand what the speaker is saying, and the ways that audiences interpret and understand are governed by language's structure. Moreover, the structure is a product of the linguistic relationships that precede it. Thus, even if a speaker doesn't mean it, an audience infers something from the use of *man* for all people or *black* as evil. Indeed, communicating to audiences is difficult because language is so slippery and because audience members bring their own predispositions to any given speech.

ETHICS, AUDIENCES, AND PUBLICS

In the movie *Star Wars,* the hero, Luke Skywalker, learns that good and evil are intertwined—that the Force, which he wants to harness for Good, has a Dark Side. In some ways, this is true of rhetoric as well. Rhetoric, as communication or persuasion, can't have good effects without the possibility of bad effects; the power to *use* rhetoric implies the power to *misuse* rhetoric. Of course, the reverse holds true as well: the ability to persuade people to do evil also implies the ability to persuade them to do good or noble things — the ethical way of using rhetoric.

In thinking about ethical approaches to rhetoric, it's helpful to identify issues that should govern the choices we make. The following issues matter the most:

- *Deception.* Deliberate deception is unethical. Sometimes speakers feel justified in deceiving the audience for its own good, but this is rarely justifiable. The Golden Rule ("Treat others as you want to be treated") applies well for matters of deception — how many of us would like to be deceived, being deprived of the chance to make a fully informed decision about an issue? Deception is also a strategic mistake; in the long run, people find out and then don't trust the speaker (see the discussion of *ethos* in Chapter 4). But it is damaging in another, more important, way: choosing to be less than fully honest demeans the speaker and reduces her moral integrity, even if no one finds out. Think about the kind of person you imagine yourself to be. Why would you choose to communicate in a way that runs against your ideals for yourself? What would that say about you? There are many forms of deception; for example:

  - *Lying by commission* involves saying or communicating something the speaker knows not to be true.

  - *Lying by omission* occurs when the speaker knowingly doesn't mention something that the audience would like to know. Often, speakers omit information unethically, such as when they don't refer to evidence against their case. If you have a good case, you shouldn't worry about counterarguments; refuting them well will make your case stronger.

  - Sometimes speakers make assertions without knowing if they are true. The philosopher Harry Frankfurt (1929–) has recently argued that this is, in his words, *bullshit*.[5] He points out that while there is often a gray area about what a speaker does or doesn't know, it's not fair to present audiences with arguments or information when they think the speaker is on solid ground, and she knows she's not.

- *Contrary evidence.* While it's wrong to mislead an audience, speakers can't appeal to "truth," per se, to decide what's ethical. In the process of persuasion, the audience often decides what's true and what isn't, since it's generally agreed that no one actually knows what the truth is — for example, What's the best tax policy? Is the defendant guilty? Should U.S. courthouses display the Ten Commandments? Should musicians tone down their language and sexuality? These issues, and many others, have good arguments on both sides. This doesn't mean that you can't make a case on a disputed issue; but when doing so, be sure to use good evidence and arguments.

- *Responsibilities.* A speaker has ethical obligations as a communicator in terms of responsibilities to all parties involved. You have responsibilities to your audience—to be fair and truthful to them. You also have a responsibility to yourself—to live up to your own standards and ideals.

- *Accountability.* If speakers have a part in making audiences, or in bringing together a public around a text or idea, then speakers must recognize that they are accountable for the kinds of audiences or publics they produce. Simply manipulating an audience to get what you want in the short term may create bigger problems in the long term. Though rhetorical study may not always show the most ethical way to relate to an audience or public, it does create a significant responsibility: the audience that you evoke and the public opinion that you encourage today are the ones that you will have to live with tomorrow.

3 Situations and Speech Types

Different situations call for different types of speeches. Consider the two excerpts below. The first one is from a speech by Knute Rockne, a famous football coach from Notre Dame, speaking to his team at halftime during a game in the 1920s:

> We're going inside of 'em, we're going outside of 'em — inside of 'em! outside of 'em! — and when we get them on the run once, we're going to keep 'em on the run. And we're not going to pass unless their secondary comes up too close. But don't forget, men — we're gonna get 'em on the run, we're gonna go, go, go, go! — and we aren't going to stop until we go over that goal line! And don't forget, men — today is the day we're gonna win. They can't lick us — and that's how it goes. . . . The first platoon men — go in there and fight, fight, fight, fight, fight! What do you say, men![1]

The next excerpt is from President George Bush's 2003 state of the union address. The president is speaking about the need for continuing support of his agenda in the war on terror:

> Our war against terror is a contest of will in which perseverance is power. In the ruins of two towers, at the western wall of the Pentagon, on a field in Pennsylvania, this nation made a pledge, and we renew that pledge tonight: Whatever the duration of this struggle and whatever the difficulties, we will not permit the triumph of violence in the affairs of men; free people will set the course of history. [2]

The speeches have some similarities: both are about overcoming an opponent, both solicit support and aim to motivate, and both remind their audiences of an obligation to exhibit a tireless will. But there are obvious differences, including the subject matter and the context.

The situation that animates a speech — the context, time, audience, and circumstances — is the **rhetorical situation**. Because speeches address specific needs for specific audiences at a given time in a given place, the rhetorical situation is key to understanding any given speech. Thinking about the rhetorical situation this way allows us to say that the style, tone, and composition of Knute Rockne's speech were very persuasive as a pep talk and that the same aspects of the president's speech matched the formality and solemnity required to persuade his national audience. Neither speech would have suited the other's audience. But how can we define the difference between the two without relying on our intuition? We might start by giving a more formal account of the rhetorical situation for each of the speeches.

In this chapter, we'll discuss the different ways of understanding the rhetorical situation. We'll focus on Aristotle's theory of situation as the place where the speech happens, Cicero's theory of situation as the intentions behind the speech, Lloyd Bitzer's idea of situation as rhetorical action in a context, and Michael Calvin McGee's idea of the rhetorical situation as a total of events, actors, and processes. Our goal will be to show why the rhetorical situation is so central to understanding a persuasive speech.

ARISTOTLE'S THREE TYPES OF SPEECHES

In ancient models, as in Aristotle's *Rhetoric,* the rhetorical situation of a speech was determined by the place where the speech was given (and, thus, its essential purpose): in front of a jury, at a funeral, or in the senate. The different locations influenced how a speaker would compose his speech. In Chapter 1, we classified these speeches as forensic, epideictic, and deliberative. Here is another explanation of these three types, including how they relate to speeches you might hear or deliver today:

- *Forensic.* *Forensic* means "pertaining to the law," so a **forensic speech** or situation is a legal one. The goal of a forensic speech is to argue guilt or innocence, and the audience is a judge, a jury, or a group of people who can render judgment. Popular television shows such as *Law & Order* (and its spin-offs), *Boston Legal, The Practice,* and *L.A. Law* have made the basic style of forensic rhetoric familiar.

- *Epideictic.* **Epideictic speeches**, often called "occasional" speeches, are usually used more at events than at specific institutions. While forensic speeches are tied to the court and deliberative speeches to a congress or legislature, epideictic speeches can range from Fourth of July orations, to eulogies, to graduation speeches or acceptance speeches. Epideictic speeches don't attempt to persuade the audience as directly as deliberative or forensic speeches do, but they do seek a judgment of quality from the audience.

- *Deliberative.* A **deliberative speech** or situation occurs when there is a need to decide about a course of future action. In the public sphere, deliberative speeches would address issues such as gay marriage, U.S. policy in the Middle East, and income tax or health care policy. Deliberative speeches assume the audience has a role, as voters or decision makers, and ask them to choose one course of action over others. In your personal life, you may use deliberative thinking when choosing an academic major or career, deciding where to live, or determining the best candidate in an election campaign.

Though these categories provide a way of talking about the rhetorical situation, reality does not always neatly fit the definitions or classifications in this system. Surely, in all of human experience there are more than three basic needs for speeches. One solution that preserved Aristotle's classifications was to add more types of speeches. Below is a brief list to give you an idea of the possibilities:

- *Eulogy*: a speech given at a funeral to commemorate a person who has died
  - These speeches often try to be "well reasoned, well said."
  - Eulogies not only praise the departed but also make sense of their passing for the audience.
- *Encomium* (plural, *encomia*): a speech that holds someone or something up as an example for others
  - These speeches praise a person or thing.
  - They rely on common values that the audience likely holds.
  - Encomia are used for encouragement, exhortation, or instruction.
- *Apologia*: a speech that justifies or apologizes for an action
  - The goal of apologia is to get the audience to view a person or action more favorably.
  - Apologia aims at proving innocence or good intention or demonstrating mitigating circumstances.
  - Apologia seeks to change judgment about the accused person or action.

This list is not comprehensive, since it would be impossible to identify all the kinds of speeches that could be given in human history. And that is a problem. Simply adding more kinds of speeches turns Aristotle's tidy system into one too messy to use. Thus, rhetoricians needed to think about the rhetorical situation in another way—one that is not dependent on an innumerable set of circumstances.

CICERO AND THE SPEAKER'S INTENT

Cicero (106–43 BCE), a Roman senator and orator, argued that rhetoric saturates every relationship—not only the relationship between speakers and audiences, but also the ones between individuals, between readers and texts, and so on. If rhetoric is present every time people communicate—indeed, if all speech is rhetorical, aimed at convincing an audience of something—then we need something more than a list of all possible interactions to define the rhetorical situation.

Cicero claimed that no matter how complex the rhetorical landscape, rhetoric has traditionally focused on certain situations and uses for communication. Here the situation is defined by the speaker's intent instead of the context that prompts the speech. In Cicero's system, speeches of all kinds are classified by their purpose: to inform, to persuade, and to entertain.[3]

- **Informational speaking** occurs when the speaker tries to help an audience understand information, often for a purpose. For Cicero, this function of rhetoric is "to teach" (*docere* in Latin). For example, a speaker might try to help a group of teens understand the dangers of AIDS and how to avoid getting it by providing them with factual information. In instances where the speaker is genuinely trying to teach or inform, it is important to be as clear and accurate as possible. Providing information does not need to be boring; speakers can adapt to their audiences by pointing out how the topic connects to them and how it might be useful to them. Sometimes speakers act as if they are just giving information when in fact they expect their information to be persuasive; when this occurs, their intentions move from teaching to persuading (see below).

- **Persuasive speaking** occurs when the speaker wants to cause a change in the audience; for Cicero, its function is "to move" (*movere* in Latin) an audience. Persuasive speaking assumes there is a difference or disagreement between the speaker and the audience. Sometimes the speaker is trying to convince the audience to change their minds, to think or understand something differently. In other cases, the speaker wants the audience to actually do—vote, buy, participate—something different.

  In general, a change in understanding precedes a change in action. For example, you'll change your favorite brand when you change your mind about the quality of its goods. However, when trying to persuade an audience, it is difficult to change them completely. There are degrees of persuasion, and speakers may not always go for the "home run" but work for smaller increments of change over many interactions. For example, speakers who want to explain the problem of global warming may not come right out and ask audience members to give up their cars and ride bikes—instead, they may simply aim at persuading the audience that global warming is a serious problem.

- **Speaking to entertain** is often ceremonial, occurring when the speaker wants to please or amuse an audience: a speech "to delight" (*delectare* in Latin). Speakers in this category might put less emphasis on content, relying instead on the ritual of the speech. For example, it's almost guaranteed that you'll hear specific ideas in a graduation speech: "the future is yours," "remember where you came from," "don't let others hold you back," "this is only the beginning of a journey." We listen to these speeches because they fulfill ceremonial expectations, not because we need to learn that the future really is ours. Wedding toasts and after-dinner speeches also fall into this category.

Unfortunately, Cicero's intervention does not provide a perfect system. For one thing, most speeches do all three things: inform, persuade, and entertain. In addition, these goals are abstract, making Cicero's system too general to help us fully understand speeches. Although Aristotle's and Cicero's classifications provide some rough guidelines, they do not fully describe all the elements of the rhetorical situation. In other words, to understand a speech, we do not simply need to know its context (as in Aristotle's classifying where a speech happens) and its purpose (as in Cicero's use of intention), but we have to examine the complex of events, persons, settings, and so on.

LOOKING BEYOND CLASSIFICATIONS

Aristotle's and Cicero's classifications served as the gold standard for thinking about speeches and rhetorical situations from Greek and Roman antiquity until the late 1960s, when some scholars started to explore the speech "situation" more thoroughly. One of the most influential was Lloyd Bitzer, who attempted to define the rhetorical situation by combining Aristotle's focus on circumstances with Cicero's focus on intentions. Finally, Michael Calvin McGee extends Bitzer's model beyond the situation to consider all the macro- and microprocesses that invest a speech with meaning.

LLOYD BITZER AND THE RHETORICAL SITUATION

Lloyd Bitzer (1928–) actually coined the phrase *the rhetorical situation*. Wanting to move beyond a definition that relied on classification, and recognizing that many different factors make a speaking occasion unique, Bitzer defined the rhetorical situation as a specific combination of exigence, audience, and constraints.[4]

- **Exigence** is the problem or occasion for change that causes someone to speak; when people engage in rhetorical speech, they often do so because they want to address a problem. An exigence might be anything from a student getting a bad grade on an assignment, to a group of people deciding that their employer provides inadequate healthcare benefits, to concerned citizens feeling that something should be done about global warming.

- **Audience** is the group of people who need to be persuaded to take action: the professor who might change the bad grade, fellow employees who might be convinced to put pressure on the employer, or a congressperson who faces a key vote on a bill relating to climate policy.

- **Constraints** are the things that stand in the way of dealing with the exigence. They can be attitudes or real structures — such as policies, laws, or economic constraints. They may be the opinion of the professor,

financial pressures on the company, or indifference toward environ-
mental problems.

Bitzer's goal in defining the rhetorical situation was to specify what makes
the occasion unique. Let's return to the chapter-opening extracts as a way of
illustrating this point. Knute Rockne's audience is his football team. The exigence is that the team needs motivation to perform in the second half, and
the constraint is that they are tired and discouraged from a difficult first half.
In President Bush's state of the union address, the audience is Congress, the
American people, and anyone else who might be watching the speech on TV.
The exigence is the difficult costs imposed by a long-term war, and the
change sought is support for the president's actions. The constraints are the
audience's substantial misgivings about going to war: fear of lost lives, moral
objections, and so on. Understanding the rhetorical situation in this way gives
speakers insight into what they might say to persuade the audience.

Bitzer's theory broadens our understanding of the rhetorical situation,
but it is not comprehensive enough. First, his model is a little narrow. There
are more things that make up the context of a speech than who the speaker is,
who is in the audience, and the roadblocks to persuasion — such as the culture it takes place in, the ways that culture views being a speaker, the ways that
culture views being an audience, and so on. For example, an audience at a
church service perceives itself differently from an audience at a political rally
or a rock concert. Second, Bitzer's model is mostly about speech; it does not
cover other kinds of rhetorical messages like images, movies, videos, and
newscasts. Third, his model argues that rhetorical discourse occurs in
response to a rhetorical situation, but this is not always the case. Bitzer claims
that there needs to be a problem that an audience already perceives, and the
existence of this problem (or exigence) gives the speaker an opportunity to
use rhetorical discourse. But sometimes speakers themselves create exigencies;
in other words, sometimes a speaker's primary task is to convince an audience
that an exigence, or problem, exists. For example, a speaker may try to persuade an uninformed audience that global warming or human rights viola-
tions are of real concern to them. These three problems (cultural differences
among audiences, a focus on speech, and the question of speakers creating
instead of responding to exigencies) limit Bitzer's conception of the rhetorical
situation.

MICHAEL McGEE AND THE CULTURAL CONTEXT

Michael Calvin McGee (1943–2002), another important contemporary
rhetorician, turned from a focus on the relationship between a speaker and an
audience toward a more global view of persuasive processes that give meaning
and sense to symbols (speeches, pictures, moving images, etc.) in a context.
McGee argued that Bitzer's definition should be expanded to include all the
elements that make up a persuasive situation, beyond the speaker, speech, and

audience. McGee's version also includes the occasion and the intended change embodied in a persuasive claim.[5] Thus, we have to focus not only on who is speaking, who is listening, and what the speaker is saying, but also on what the speaker is doing, where and when he is trying to get it done, and for what reasons.

McGee argued that to fully understand the rhetorical situation, a rhetorician needs to understand the culture it takes place in. This requires attention to the ways that the culture understands what it means to be a speaker (Is the speaker always one person? What about the media and other kinds of rhetorical communication?). It also requires attention to what serves as speech and what it means to be a member of an audience (Is the audience gathered in front of the speaker, intently listening; or is the speech on a TV droning on in the background?). In the traditional models that we have discussed, from Aristotle to Bitzer, the goal of **rhetorical criticism** is to read an object (a speech or a text) in the light of its surroundings. McGee expanded this approach by acknowledging persuasive processes that precede and move beyond a speech, mostly including the cultural, ideological, and political predispositions that make up audiences and messages.

McGee's theory sees rhetorical criticism not as an object but as a process. This is, in part, why scholars like McGee have argued for a broad conception of the rhetorical situation beyond speech, speaker, and audience. Equally important are the context that these elements work in, and all the processes of persuasion that lead up to the presentation to an audience. Speeches do not differ just because different people deliver them in different ways or for different purposes; they also differ because they address the concrete needs of a given situation and are constrained by audience expectations. Some rhetoricians call this concept **genre**, which is another way of saying that different types of speeches work better in different situations.

An expanded conception of the rhetorical situation helps us better understand not only what makes speeches different but also why, for example, the same speech might succeed or fail with the same audience on different occasions. Drawing on Bitzer's model, one would assume that differences in the situation affect a speaker's choice of words and key ideas. Drawing also from McGee's model, one would consider whether the tone, word choices, and delivery are **appropriate** to the situation—not just in the sense of meeting an audience's expectations, but also in the sense that cultural processes teach people what to expect from a situation and a speaker.

The idea of appropriate speech has a long history in rhetoric (see Chapter 2), stemming from the early Greek use of the term *prepon,* meaning "fitting" or "apt." Thus, both Bitzer and McGee acknowledged the importance of aptness, or appropriate fit. For example, "our war against terror is a contest of will . . . and we renew that pledge tonight" sounds more appropriate to a state of the union address than "and don't forget, men—today is the day we're gonna win. . . . Fight, fight, fight, fight, fight!" Even though you could ask a football team to "renew that pledge" of will in a halftime speech and you could say "today is the day we're gonna win" in addressing the war on terror, the tone of either speech is appropriate only for itself.

But different situations do not only require different word choices, different genres, or even wholly different speeches. They also require different speakers—not just in a literal sense, but also in the way speakers act, present themselves, and deliver their speeches. Different situations also require different audiences (see Chapter 2)—not just in terms of demographics (age, sex, race, gender, etc.), but also in terms of expectations for audience interaction (stand up and cheer at a rally; clap politely at a lecture) and levels of direct engagement (a presentation in person; a remote broadcast or a videotape).

In sum, the rhetorical situation includes considerations of who the speakers are, what they are saying, who the audience is, what the context is, why the speech is happening, and what goals and interests all sides bring to the table. The rhetorical situation is the background for any given speech that determines whether it is fitting and persuasive or inappropriate and unsuccessful.

PART II
Rhetoric in Action

Argument and Persuasion 4

As we discussed in Part I, rhetoric seeks to describe certain kinds of communication — communication designed to influence other people's thinking and action. You can try to influence others in several different ways, but if you leave out force or threats, you are left with persuasion — talking to people. Rhetoric is an explanation of how this kind of persuasion works. Many people assume that rhetoric or persuasion is the study of psychological tricks, ways of "getting" people to change their minds without thinking. In general, nothing could be further from the truth. While rhetoric certainly has a dark side that deals in tricks and deceptions (see "Ethics, Audiences, and Publics" in Chapter 2), the systematic study of rhetoric generally ignores these techniques, in part because they are *not* very systematic or reliable.

In this chapter, we will focus on the systematic and reasoned methods for changing people's minds. If you can't force people to do things, your best hope is to show them that, by their own standards, something is reasonable to do or believe. Most versions of rhetoric often take place in something like a democratic context, in which audience members are encouraged to make up their own minds by deciding between competing arguments. The speaker assumes equality with listeners; they have the right to make decisions based on what they perceive as the best reasons. Of course, communicating the best reasons is not always simple. This is why much of rhetorical practice focuses on argumentation — ways of finding and providing reasons for audiences. By considering how to discover arguments and make them persuasive, and even how they can be incorrect, we will outline and discuss the building blocks and different methods of argumentative persuasion.

PROOFS: WAYS OF BEING PERSUASIVE

Think about a recent decision you made, whether it was purchasing music or deciding what class to take or whom to date. If you think through what led up to your choice, you'll probably notice that different kinds of factors played into your decision. You may have read reviews of the music, looked through the requirements for your major, or thought hard about the pros and cons of the romantic relationship. Or you may have listened to the advice of a trusted friend or mentor. Or you may have "gone with your gut," trusting your feelings about each decision. In fact, you probably mixed all three together: the reasonable, the personal, and the emotional factors. When speakers attempt to persuade audiences, they mobilize similar resources: to elicit a change from audiences by rational means, speakers need to offer reasons for deciding between competing points of view, providing audience members with a case for why they should change their minds or actions.

We'll call anything that serves this function a **proof**, the ways of making speech persuasive. As discussed in Chapter 1, Aristotle originally classified proofs in three kinds, based on whether they originate in the speech (*logos*), the speaker (*ethos*), or the listener (*pathos*). Aristotle's analysis has been influential for 2,500 years because it explains the deep structure of the elements of persuasion. It's customary, as in other points of rhetorical theory, to use the ancient Greek terms for the proofs (*pisteis*) because this defines them more precisely. Let's take a closer look at each type of proof.

LOGOS

The **logos** of a speech is its logic; that is, the arguments it makes. In many cases, a speech tries to move an audience from one belief to another by walking the audience through reasonable steps. Aristotle identified two main kinds of reasoning to do this: formal reasoning and nonformal reasoning. Formal reasoning works by means of arguments called **syllogisms**, in which two true **premises** (propositions or statements) validly imply a third statement, the conclusion of the argument. For example:

Premise:	All students take courses.
Premise:	All who take courses get grades.
Conclusion:	All students get grades.

In a valid formal argument, if the first two premises are true then they imply the conclusion because if they are true then the conclusion *has* to be true. The conclusion is, in a sense, restating information that is already hidden in the two premises:

Premise:	All students work for grades.
Premise:	Some of those who work for grades are tempted to cheat.
Conclusion:	Some students are tempted to cheat.

Premise:	Some students study hard.
Premise:	No one who studies hard wants to fail.
Conclusion:	Some students don't want to fail.

In these cases, of course, all the statements seem obviously true; but in more complicated examples, formal reasoning can lead to surprising conclusions:

Premise:	No student wants to fail.
Premise:	Some who don't want to fail study hard.
Conclusion:	Some students don't study hard.

Do you notice something peculiar? In fact, this is not a valid argument. Even if the first two statements are true, that doesn't guarantee the conclusion is true; this becomes evident if you think about the fact that the "some" who don't want to fail might not be students. Formal logic has advantages and disadvantages; it can prove statements pretty conclusively, but it can also be confusing and hard to follow.

Enthymemes

As a rhetorical alternative to the syllogism, Aristotle proposed two methods of reasoning/argument that can be adapted to persuade audiences: enthymemes and examples.

Aristotle called legitimately persuasive arguments that weren't formally valid **enthymemes**. These involve good reasoning but are missing some steps in the logic. Enthymemes are parallel to syllogisms, but simpler and more flexible. An example might be:

Bob is a student, therefore Bob is registered for courses.

You can leave out the step "All students register for courses" if everyone in your audience will know it. This is a key feature of enthymemes; they are transparent for only their target audience, since they take advantage of audience knowledge. For example, suppose you were told:

Obviously they won't be singing barbershop, since they're using a piano.

The inference here wouldn't be obvious or make sense to you unless you knew, as a musician would, that for technical reasons barbershop singers can't use a piano as accompaniment. This enthymeme would be clear only to an audience with that knowledge.

Some enthymemes rely on commonly accepted patterns of reasoning. Here are some examples:

- *Signs* involve one thing indicating another: smoke implies fire, dark clouds imply rain, or previous immoral behavior implies current immoral behavior. ("He's lied before, so he'll do it again.")

- *Cause and effect* enthymemes occur in arguments about the consequences of things or actions, such as the dangers of experimenting with drugs or risky sexual behavior. ("We know a lot of kids who have flunked because of too much partying.")

- *Analogies* compare seemingly different things, as in arguments that try to show the futility of the current "war on drugs" by comparing it to Prohibition. ("A college education is like money in the bank.")

Examples

In contrast to the reasoning of enthymemes, **examples** (*paradeigmata*) are a specific kind of rhetorical argument that speakers use to prove their claims through **inductive reasoning**—a type of reasoning that assumes that if something is true in specific cases, then it's true in general. In a speech where you are arguing that a military draft would be unpopular in the United States, you would want to cite examples of previous unpopular drafts as part of your proof. Examples are an important way in which arguments get adapted to audiences, since examples can be chosen to be very specific to the audience. If you choose examples that aren't familiar to or understood by your audience, the examples won't be able to perform their persuasive function as proof. If you were speaking to students in, say, a prison school program instead of a traditional college setting, examples about dormitory life, student organizations, or weekend frivolity wouldn't be very effective.

Examples can be real or hypothetical, depending on what your argumentative resources/needs are, but both types help speakers argue to a specific audience:

- *Real examples* are things from your own experience or research that illustrate or support the claim you're making. If you're arguing that AIDS education programs work, you'll need to cite examples of specific programs and how they've been effective.

- *Hypothetical examples* are made-up examples. Speakers need these when there aren't appropriate real examples or when they need something to connect to the audience better than a real example could. Suppose you're arguing about problems with the death penalty. You can cite examples of people who were wrongly convicted, but you might wonder if your audience will just dismiss them as criminals. Instead, you can invent a plausible example ("What if a student, just like you, were in the wrong place at the wrong time?") to illustrate the limitations of the justice system.

ETHOS

Argument is not the only dimension of persuasive proof. You might sometimes hear what sound like strong arguments, yet be inclined to doubt them. To accept someone's argument is, in a sense, to trust that person, so audiences make judgments about the speaker. Audiences ask questions (such as "What kind of person is this?) to evaluate the speaker and decide if she is credible and whether to change their mind about the topic at hand. This is the same as asking, "What kind of *ethos* does this person have?"

When audiences wonder about the speaker's **ethos**, they are considering his credibility (believability) and trustworthiness. *Ethos* is a Greek term that can have two meanings: "character" and "habit." These two meanings are related, since a person's character is composed of habits, the things that a person just "does" all the time. A dishonest person is one who habitually lies, while an honest person is one who habitually tells the truth. A brave person is one who, by habit, does courageous things, while a coward is someone who routinely shrinks in the face of danger. When you think about whether to believe a speaker, to find her credible, you make a judgment about her character — is she truthful? reasonable? fair-minded?

To gain an audience's trust, persuasive speakers try to create a certain kind of relationship with their audience. Speakers create ethos in a number of ways:

- *Action.* Speakers might call explicitly on the history of their actions, as politicians often do when invoking their voting records.

- *Deeds.* Speakers might point out deeds that exemplify their character, perhaps a war record or participation in a social movement.

- *Understanding.* Speakers can show they understand their audience's point of view by adapting carefully to them, identifying similarities in their experiences and beliefs.

- *Expertise.* Speakers often claim some kind of expertise, which they can justify by citing their education or the research they have done with experts.

Ethos is not automatic. Think about cases where you weren't persuaded by a speaker; if you felt the speaker wasn't honest or didn't have your best interests in mind, you might have decided not to listen to all the (potentially good) arguments presented to you. What if the speaker asks the audience to think she is an expert on some topic and "take her word for" some of the facts or arguments? Without the appropriate ethos (demonstrating the relevant education or experience to the audience), listeners might not grant the speaker what she wants.

PATHOS

Audiences come to a speech with feelings based on anticipation, and these feelings are transformed, or not, by the speech. **Pathos** refers to the emotional state of the audience, as produced by the speaker or speech. The audience may feel bored, irritated, or excited by the speaker or speech. Or they may have vague or specific feelings about the topic. The important thing is that their feelings (what Aristotle calls their "state of mind") help frame how they understand the arguments of the speech and whether they may accept them. Successful speakers work to bring the audiences' emotions into alignment with the arguments they are making.

For example, students may go to a required presentation on vivisection (cutting or operating on live animals for scientific research) not knowing or caring much about it. However, this type of animal experimentation tends to evoke strong feelings in people, depending on how it is presented. Sometimes the presentation focuses on the pain of human disease, and how much animal experimentation can help; sometimes it focuses on the suffering or exploitation of the animals in the experiments. In either case, the speaker assumes that the arguments she presents are going to be interpreted with an emotional response. So the speaker will try to get the audience's emotions in line with the conclusion she wants them to reach. For example, if you think that a new law is needed to solve a problem, you would want the audience members to think the problem was serious and scary; even if you have lots of evidence, if the audience doesn't feel it's important, your evidence may not matter to them.

Speakers address pathos partly by choosing language and metaphors that convey emotion, and partly by choosing examples and illustrations that are familiar to audience members, allowing them to "see" what the problem is. In the case of animal experimentation, one presentation will use the term *victim*s for the people suffering from a disease, while another will use it for the animals in the experiments. As long as each argument backs up the use of this term (proving there is unjustified suffering), it is not manipulative but a way of letting emotion reinforce logic. It's possible, of course, to go too far and present images or information so horrifying that the audience feels traumatized and literally or figuratively turns away. Attempts to manipulate people directly with emotion are seldom successful. The most effective use of pathos puts it in harmony with the other proofs. While in the end it is usually the speaker's arguments that determine whether the audience changes its mind, it is the audience's feelings that frame those arguments.

TOPOI: TOOLS FOR DISCOVERING ARGUMENTS

In the classical tradition of rhetoric, persuasion depends on some kind of argument. A persuader will need an ample supply of arguments because if he can't think of ways to argue, he can't persuade. So anyone trained in persuasion has to be skilled at creating or *finding* arguments on almost any topic.

In rhetoric, **topoi** are the general forms that arguments take, regardless of their actual content. The Greek word *topos* means "place" (plural, *topoi*), which is why, for example, we call maps that show geographical features *topographical* maps. Just as we can talk about the *topography,* the places or features of land, we can also talk about common places for thinking about argument.

The Greeks thought that arguments were, in a sense, spread out in space, and if a speaker knew his way around that space, he would be able to find the ones he needed. The better the speaker knew the landscape of argument, the more easily he could create persuasive appeals. The study of rhetoric could make a speaker just as familiar with the inventory of arguments in politics, policy, and law as with more ordinary subjects.

To take an ordinary case, suppose you are planning dinner with friends and are trying to persuade one another about where to go. At this point, before knowing anything about you, your friends, or the local restaurants, we could determine a few possible arguments—for example, whether the restaurant:

- is more or less expensive
- has a better or worse reputation
- serves ethnic food or comfort food
- is new or tried and true

Thinking about these potential arguments could lead to a conversation like this:

> "Let's try someplace new."
> "No, it might be terrible and we'd waste our money. Let's go for something cheap."
> "But inexpensive restaurants are often bad."
> "I'm craving ethnic food."
> "But I'm in the mood for comfort food."

The comments above are really topoi, general places to find specific lines of arguments. So, whether you're arguing about where to go to dinner or what the best response to terrorism is, you'll still go through a similar process, looking for the possible arguments, even though the content of the arguments will change. You may not realize it, but you already knew what many of these topoi are.

GENERAL TOPOI

Classical rhetoricians identify some topoi (the *koinoi topoi,* common topics or commonplaces) as completely general and applicable to any situation or context. These topoi are helpful because they apply in many different types of arguments. But it takes great skill to use them, since you have to connect these very general ideas to your specific situation. The following are some types of general topoi (the last example in each shows how you can look for different arguments using the same issue — in this case, asking a teacher to change a grade):

- *More and less likely.* If the more likely thing does not happen, the less likely thing will also not happen.
  - "If the expensive restaurant is not good, then the cheaper version won't be good either."
  - "Since I can't afford a used car, I certainly can't afford a new car."
  - "This is easier than the last assignment; if I was capable of an A there, I should be capable of an A on this one."
- *Consistency of motives.* If a person has a reason to do something, he or she probably will do it.
  - "Bob didn't eat at that restaurant; he must have known something."

- "All politicians take whatever they can get away with."
- "Amy wants to make Honor Roll, I'll bet she's studying hard."
- *Hypocrisy.* If standards apply to one person, they should apply to another.
  - "Well, you also don't give restaurants a second chance if they weren't good the first time you ate there."
  - "You can't tell me not to smoke, since you do."
  - "You've always said that we have to exercise charity in interpreting others' arguments; perhaps some charity would help here?"
- *Analogy.* If things are alike in an obvious way, they will also be alike in other ways.
  - "This place is owned by the same people as our favorite restaurant; it's probably just as good."
  - "Your body is like a machine, so it must also need fuel."
  - "This is the same type of assignment as the previous one; I should be capable of the same score."

Not all of these are equally good in every situation; that will depend on the audience, available evidence, and so forth. But the more arguments you can generate, the more choices you have in persuading your audience.

Suppose you are arguing about a policy, claiming that one course of action is better than another and showing that it is different, in a good way, from the alternatives; the action could be choosing a restaurant or choosing an anti-terrorism policy. You would make comparisons to establish the differences: one issue has greater importance or magnitude than the other ("Preventing terrorism is more important than protecting civil rights."), one choice will cause bad or good outcomes ("If we go to the student union to eat, we might have to wait in line."), one issue is a part of a larger issue ("What kind of society is the government protecting from terrorists if it does not respect civil rights?"), or one potential outcome of the choice is more important than other potential outcomes ("Sure, we'll get a good meal at the fancy French restaurant, but it will bankrupt us."). If your decision-making is guided by the best argument, topoi will help you generate a number of possible arguments to evaluate to find the best one.

SPECIAL TOPOI

Some topics apply only in special contexts; these are the *idioi topoi,* or special topics. These concern subjects about which people often argue. What are the contexts to which special topics apply? Aristotle identified five subjects and standard lines of argument for each. Here are Aristotle's topics, with a current example from each side of an issue:

- *Finances.* The public funding of the government:
  - "We don't want the government to waste our money, so we should hold taxes to a minimum."
  - "We do want the government to provide us services, so we should pay enough taxes and monitor how the money is spent."

- *War and peace.* The government and issues about diplomacy:
  - "A war in self-defense is a just war."
  - "Wars shouldn't do more harm than good."

- *National defense.* Issues about the military:
  - "A strong standing army prevents problems."
  - "The resources put into a standing army would be better spent on social programs."

- *Imports and exports.* The government's trade policy:
  - "Tariffs and taxes should support businesses here at home."
  - "The freest trade benefits the most people."

- *The framing of law.* The workings of elected representatives:
  - "Political advertising allows lobbyists to influence legislation too much."
  - "The interests that lobbyists represent are also voters' interests."

Aristotle developed these subject areas for the political environment in ancient Greece. In contemporary America, we can add additional categories that are important to us. For example, it's common for people to use a topos of government waste ("The government always wastes money, so it's best to limit the amount we give to it."). This topos can be applied in many different ways according to the context and circumstances, but it still stands as an available resource for arguers. Of course, there is a counter-topos ("You get what you pay for," or "TNSTAAFL: there's no such thing as a free lunch."), which emphasizes that people won't get services from the government that they don't pay for.

A skillful rhetorician knows how to quickly generate arguments on a given topic by looking in familiar places — that is, by considering the topoi. Not everything generated will be high quality or persuasive; some arguments may need to be discarded, and some may have to be filled out with research. But a strong command of the topoi allows a speaker to have a number of choices about which arguments to present.

STOCK ISSUES

Every argument focuses on a specific subject. When a speaker argues something to an audience, he assumes that there are (at least) two sides — otherwise there is nothing to argue about. Any point on which people could take different sides is an **issue**. If the issue is gun control, there are (at least) two sides: for legal controls, and against legal controls. If the issue is prayer in the public schools, one side wants it, and the other side doesn't. When two arguments meet head-on over an issue, rhetoricians call it **clash**, or *achieving clash*. In practice, achieving clash can be quite difficult; like two ships passing in the night, people frequently argue past each other. If they're not arguing about the same issue (or subissue), they're not actually engaging the other side and are unlikely to make progress. For example, the issue of gun control has at least two subissues:

- Is it legal for the U.S. government to restrict gun ownership?
- Does widespread gun ownership result in increased death and violence?

Each is a legitimate and important part of the overall debate about guns. Yet if one side is talking about the Second Amendment (legality) and the other about crime statistics for Washington, D.C. (violence), they are talking past each other, and are not achieving clash. For their dialogue to be productive, they should first argue about one of these points and then the other.

In special contexts, particularly in legal and political or policy contexts, the issues of an argument can be known in advance. These are called **stock issues** because they are the standardized issues in that context. Each side knows what issues the other side will have to address and can anticipate its arguments. But before we examine the stock issues, we have to explain the framework for policy and legal argument: presumption and burden of proof.

PRESUMPTION AND BURDEN OF PROOF

Once two sides engage on an issue, they begin to argue. Sometimes arguing about an issue leads the two sides to a stalemate, at which point each party just contradicts the other: "Yes, it is — No, it isn't. Yes, it is — No, it isn't. Yes, it is — No, it isn't." When there is, so to speak, a tie between the sides, then the argument has no outcome, no decision is reached, and no action gets taken. In these situations, there is a practical need to come to a decision and bring closure to the debate; even deciding against taking action is a decision. Two common rhetorical contexts that require a decision to be made are (1) trials (legal issues), and (2) debates over a law or *policy*.

To address this problem, the concepts of presumption and burden of proof come into play. Although normally applied to law and politics, they can apply in other contexts as well. **Presumption** is a tie-breaking principle, a prior decision about which side should be given the benefit of the doubt in the case of a tie. You're probably most familiar with presumption in the law, from the formula "presumed innocent until proven guilty."

What is the purpose of this principle? Suppose that you have been put on trial for stealing a bicycle, and that each side has the same amount of evidence or proof. What happens next? The prosecution and defense can't go on arguing forever, and the court either has to punish you or let you go. (Or, for another example, when members of Congress debate a bill, they either have to pass it, enacting a law, or reject it.)

In practice, presumption works like this. Your defense starts with how things are right now, before you begin arguing. This state of affairs is the **status quo** (literally, "what stands [now]"). A legal argument focuses on changing the status quo. Before anyone accused you, the status quo was that you were innocent of any crime, including stealing a bike. When you're accused, the police or district attorney are making a case that your status should be changed from innocent to guilty. But the status quo always has presumption, which means that in the case of equal amounts of evidence on both sides, you are presumed to be innocent.

Another way of understanding this point is that the police have the **burden of proof**, which is the other side of the coin from presumption: your accusers have to prove you are guilty, but you don't have to prove you are innocent (because you are presumed to be innocent). Many people misunderstand this principle, mostly because legal television shows don't always get it right. Since the prosecution (the police or district attorney) has the burden of proof, all you have to argue is that it hasn't proved its case, which is quite different from arguing that you're innocent. To do so, you can point out that the prosecution's only witness is unreliable, which doesn't show that you didn't steal the bike—only that they haven't proved you did. These principles mean that the two sides involved in a case don't go into an argument as equals; those on the side of the status quo have an advantage.

This works similarly in a legislative context. The status quo is how the government is doing things right now. Then someone notices a problem—maybe too many bicycles are being stolen—and proposes a law to solve the problem. Those who propose the change are the *affirmative* side (they affirm the change), and those who argue against it are the *negative* side (they oppose the change). Who has presumption here? Since the status quo is the state of things without the new law, the affirmative side has the burden of proof, and presumption goes to the negative side. The negative doesn't need to argue that there's anything good about the status quo, just that the affirmative hasn't done a good enough job in making its case.

The advantage to the status quo makes sense in both contexts. Presumption is an essentially conservative principle, since it ensures that a controversy has a real outcome and that should a mistake be made, it errs to the side of caution, "giving the benefit of the doubt." In the legal case, a mistake would involve either convicting an innocent person or letting a criminal go free. Because it seems much worse to punish an innocent person than to let a guilty person go, presumption shifts argumentative power in favor of the defendant. Additionally, the government is more powerful than an accused individual; the police have many more resources for gathering evidence than you do — even if you hire a lawyer, you still can't quite match them. So presumption helps balance the government's advantage.

In the policy context, presumption makes sense because even though we all might want a problem solved, we don't want to make the situation worse. And experience shows that it's very easy to make things worse. Any policy might not only fail to solve the problem, it might even make the original problem worse (this is called a *perverse outcome*) or create other problems as bad as the original problem (these are called the *disadvantages*). Since those who propose a law or policy have the burden of proof, disadvantages are unlikely to occur. The arguments against the affirmative should bring out most of the problems with the proposal, and if evidence is equal on both sides, it's better to reject the proposal and start over with one that can clearly meet the burden of proof.

LEGAL STOCK ISSUES

In legal contexts, the standard issues, or points of clash, are classified by Fact, Definition, and Value and are represented by questions:

- *Fact: What happened?* What are the facts of the case? Was something stolen? Was someone harmed? Was a particular person present on a given day and time? Who saw what? When? Where?

- *Definition: What was it?* How should the act be classified or defined? For example, if something is stolen, the act might be theft, burglary, assault, grand theft, petty theft, or something else. For legal purposes, it makes a difference how the wrongful action is classified.

- *Value: What should be done?* What values have to be weighed in deciding a penalty? Are there any extenuating circumstances? Does anything mitigate (lessen) the wrong that was done? Is any public purpose served by punishing or not punishing the accused person?

From television programs like *Law & Order* and *CSI,* you may be familiar with the ways that each side (prosecution and defense) will address a point of clash, with either testimony ("Yes, I saw him there.") or circumstantial evidence ("Tests show the presence of his DNA at the crime scene."). Stock issues allow attorneys to develop not only arguments but also rebuttals to the arguments their opponents will likely make. Strong arguers, in any context, ensure they clearly understand the issues when they begin to design a speech.

POLICY STOCK ISSUES

Policy argument has its own set of stock issues. Policy argument begins with a *resolution,* or a statement of the new policy ("Resolved: The city will implement a .5 percent sales tax increase for the purpose of funding new computers for all public schools."). Since under the status quo there is no such policy, argument begins with the affirmative side — those who want a change; the negative side then tries to show that the affirmative hasn't made its case. Here are the stock issues of policy argument; the questions are those that the affirmative will have to answer to make its case.

- *Significance.* Is the problem significant? Who is harmed? How much are they harmed? In our example, the affirmative would have to show that outdated or missing computer equipment is severely harming the education of students. The negative might counter that this is just inconvenient to students, not actually harming their education.

- *Inherence.* Is the cause of the problem inherent in the status quo? Is the cause of the problem rooted in current policy rather than something else? The negative might argue that test scores are declining because the district's population is changing, not because of outdated or missing computers.

- *Plan.* The affirmative has to outline a consistent plan and show how it would implement that plan. The negative may point out inconsistencies in the plan or obstacles to its implementation.

- *Solvency.* The affirmative has to show that the plan actually solves the problem — that the tax increase will generate enough money to purchase the computers that will improve student learning. The negative may point out that student performance might lag anyway or that the money might not be spent appropriately.

- *Disadvantages.* The affirmative must argue that the plan doesn't create a problem worse than the one it is supposed to solve. The negative may question this point — claiming, for example, that the focus on computers draws attention away from the real problem: teacher incompetence.

For each of these issues, the negative will try to show that the affirmative has not met its burden of proof; the negative doesn't have to show that a policy is bad or wrong, just that (by the principle of presumption) the affirmative has shown insufficient reason to change.

Most legislative and parliamentary debate follows, more or less, the logic of these issues; they are also the basis of most competitive high school and college debating in the United States. If you have mastered these issues, you will be able to easily navigate even complex public issues.

FALLACIES

One problem with persuasion is that whether speakers intend to or not, they can make mistakes in their arguments and end up with incorrect conclusions they didn't earn through valid argument. In the study of rhetoric, we apply the term **fallacies** to mistakes and errors in argumentation and reasoning. Fallacious arguments are invalid because even though the conclusions appear to follow from the premises, they actually don't. A fallacious argument involves a *non sequitur,* which is Latin for "it does not follow," meaning that (1) the conclusion isn't implied by the evidence, or (2) the argument's reasons do not support its claim, making the argument invalid. If an audience notices your fallacies, you will lose credibility and fail to persuade them. In this way, fallacies can damage your ethos.

While no argument is perfect or airtight, many contain obvious and iden-tifiable errors in reasoning. Part of rhetorical skill involves being able to rec-ognize fallacies — to know and reject poor reasoning and to make sure that you as a speaker don't use it. Here are some common types of fallacies; many were systematized by scholars during the Renaissance and are still known by their Latin names:

- *Ad personam* ("to the person," or *ad hominem,* "to the man"). Instead of focusing on the argument, the speaker makes judgments or personal attacks about the person(s) advancing the opposite side of the argument. An example would be arguing that Senator Jones's vote on the tax policy bill is wrong because he drinks alcohol excessively and has affairs with young women. While Senator Jones's behavior may be frowned upon, his tax policy vote is independent of that behavior.

- *Ad populum* ("to the people"). This error is also known as the band-wagon effect, whereby the speaker argues that "if it's popular and lots of people believe it, it must be true." But lots of widely believed things aren't true. Did your parents ever ask you, "If everyone were jumping off a cliff, would you do it also?" The same reasoning applies in argumenta-tion. Just because many people believe something doesn't mean it's true and doesn't make it sound reasoning for an argument.

- *Appeal to authority* (*ad verecundiam,* "to respectfulness"). Arguments often depend on the knowledge of experts, but there are appropriate and inappropriate experts depending on the argument. An appropriate authority has recognized expertise in the subject of the argument. In a fallacious appeal to authority, someone with a PhD in engineering might be presented as an expert on other issues such as trade subsidies or globalization.

- *Appeal to ignorance.* The burden of proof lies with the originators of an argument. If they do not meet their burden of proof, then the argument becomes an appeal to ignorance, and therefore fallacious. For example, some people may argue that "UFOs and aliens exist, because no one has definitely proved they don't." There might be, in fact, some good argu-ments for both sides of this issue. But this isn't one of them, since the lack of proof doesn't by itself constitute proof.

- *Guilt by association.* This mistake occurs when an arguer jumps to conclusions based on evidence that is irrelevant to the point at issue. Stereotyping is a common example of guilt by association. For example, the statements "This is a bad law because it was proposed by a Republican" and "This policy is weak because Democrats support it" are fallacies. The merits of the law or the policy have to be argued on their own, not based on their connection to something or someone else.

- *Post hoc ergo propter hoc* ("after this, therefore because of this"). This fallacy involves faulty cause-and-effect reasoning. An argument about cause and effect has to show that two things occur together and are actually connected. Consider the connection between eating excessively and gaining weight; they occur together, and it's possible to explain the mechanism by which extra calories translate into extra weight. However, this type of reasoning becomes a fallacy when arguers make a causal claim based only on things occurring together instead of proving the connection. For example, every morning the sun rises and you get a day older, but you can't infer from that information alone that the sun's rising caused you to get older. Similarly, there is a correlation between poverty and poor school performance. Does that mean that poverty causes kids to do poorly in school? No. Although some factors linked to poverty may well be the causes of poor performance, an arguer can't jump immediately from correlation to cause; the real cause may not be poverty itself but some other factor associated with poverty.

- *Red herring.* As noted above, arguers try to achieve clash to stay on point, but it can be very difficult to sort out the issues and stay on track even when everyone is trying to do so. Sometimes a speaker deliberately takes the argument off point, and that is the red herring fallacy. (Why the odd term *red herring*? In earlier times, when prisoners escaped from jails they would drag fish across their trails and then throw them into the brush, to throw off the dogs pursuing them.) This error occurs when an arguer changes the issues so that they are irrelevant to the argument being presented. For example, in an argument about the social effects of pornography and whether it should remain legal, someone might interrupt with, "Well, adult stores ruin downtown businesses." Whether or not that is true, it takes things in a different direction (that of financial issues), away from the original issue of the social implications of legalized pornography.

- *Slippery slope.* This fallacy presents a chain of cause and effect whereby the first cause establishes an irreversible trend, sometimes called the domino effect. When setting up an argument, a speaker needs to establish every single link in the chain; if the speaker implies that the links are there without actually defending each one, it becomes a fallacy. For example, imagine someone arguing that the use of alcohol leads to the use of other, harder drugs: alcohol leads to smoking pot, pot to pills, pills to methamphetamines (meth), and meth to cocaine or heroin. Therefore, society has to stop people from drinking so they won't become heroin addicts. While many good arguments exist against the use of alcohol and marijuana, this isn't one of them because there is no evidence of a causal connection between the use of alcohol and the use of hard drugs.

CHALLENGING TRADITIONAL RHETORIC

The American rhetorician Kenneth Burke (1897–1993), who began writing about rhetoric in the 1930s, offered an alternative account of persuasion. Burke's perspective on rhetoric is extremely complex and difficult, but he is a major influence on contemporary thought about persuasion. His account of rhetoric was the first serious challenge to the tradition of Cicero and Aristotle; he moved rhetoric away from a civic context and understood it as the primary force in human social life. According to Burke, everything we do with others — cooperate, love, hate, fight, organize, and so on — we do through rhetoric.

KENNETH BURKE AND A NEW DEFINITION OF RHETORIC

Burke began with five assumptions, which are contained in his essay "Definition of Man." By "man," Burke meant all humans, and he wanted to identify the fundamental way in which humans, as social beings, are bound to each other and motivated by the features of language and rhetoric. Burke didn't see rhetoric as something added on to the functions of daily language, but rather as something embodied within ordinary communication practices. Rhetoric, said Burke, "is rooted in an essential function of language itself, a function that is wholly realistic and continually born anew: the use of language as a symbolic means of inducing cooperation in beings that by nature respond to symbols."[1] Each of Burke's five assumptions describes a characteristic of human beings that makes them different from animals.

1. Humans are the symbol-making, symbol-using, and symbol-misusing animal.

When human beings think, they think in symbols. Symbols include not only language but also images and much more: buildings, colors, hairstyles, ways of walking—all could be symbols, though most of them do not form a language suitable for thinking. Burke emphasized that there is no natural way to think or represent the world, no simple reflection of "the way things are."

Symbols — languages — are created by people and are used by people. In addition, symbols are "misused" by people, who can play with language for humorous, ironic, or artistic reasons; many jokes depend on using words in unusual ways, and poetry usually departs from ordinary language usage.

2. Humans are the inventor of the negative.

Languages or symbol systems are more than one-to-one representations between words and things; symbol systems create more possibilities than that. In particular, they create the possibility of things that are *not,* things that don't or can't exist. This can range from trivial things like unicorns and comic-book heroes to important things like utopian societies that groups may be working toward but haven't yet achieved. Burke pointed out that people can talk about (symbolize) things they have never done, and that an important part of social regulation consists of prohibitions on behavior, or learning *not* to do things. He called this idea the great "Thou Shalt Not," and it is only possible through the medium of language to imagine an action and then decide (or tell others) not to do it. Thus, the idea of good (what one should do) and evil (what one should not do) is made possible by language, created in and through human social interactions.

3. Humans are separated from their natural condition by instruments of their own making.

Burke regarded humans' natural condition as their animal nature, controlled by desires and emotions. What makes human different from animals is the ability to think and decide using language and symbols. But, to an extent, the possibilities for how we humans think are constrained by the language we speak. And so while we make decisions, the terms on which we think about them may not be within our control. For example, most Americans eat meat, but they seldom think about the meats they *don't* eat. In English, for some animals, we have a different word for the flesh we consume:

Pig = pork
Cow = beef
Sheep = mutton
Deer = venison
Chicken = poultry

This marks out, roughly, the animals we eat, for we call them by a different name when they are food. But in our symbolic world, there are other edible animals (such as dogs and cats) that aren't part of the category "food" and thus do not have a different name as food. Did you have to learn that, or did it never occur to you since no one ever talked about them that way? Language shapes our thinking even as we use language to think.

4. *Humans are goaded by the spirit of hierarchy.*

Burke's theory of language is also a theory of motivation, an explanation for why people are moved to act (or not). Symbols create systems of categories, and Burke claimed that along with every set of categories, people create value judgments. Once people distinguish between, say, different colors of hair, they decide that some colors are "better" than others and thereby create a hierarchy of colors. For Burke, this is a fundamental human trait, and for the most part these hierarchies are embedded in our language. Short/tall, fat/thin, rich/poor, city/country, East Coast/West Coast, Democrat/Republican, Catholic/Protestant/Jewish/Islamic/Buddhist/Hindu/atheist — all imply values. This doesn't mean that everyone, even within a language or culture, agrees about every hierarchy. But it does mean that people want to perceive themselves as better, rather than worse, on whatever hierarchies they find relevant. This is where rhetoric comes in. In some cases, a rhetorical appeal references a value that people find important, and it confirms to them that they are valuable. In other cases, rhetoric can explain to people why, even though they seem to rank low, they or their characteristics have value. It can be as simple as this:

> *Becky:*   Wow, you got a new car.
> *John:*   Yeah, it's not that great, but I couldn't afford anything better.
> *Becky:*   But you have low payments and get good gas mileage.

Here John's initial reaction is to say that on the hierarchy of "status" cars, he ranks pretty low. Becky introduces a different hierarchy, practicality, and points out that John looks pretty good on that score. Burke's insight was that John is motivated to accept Becky's story about economy because it makes him feel better about his decision in buying the car. In general, according to Burke, we seek out and identify with symbols — and the stories and representations created by symbols — that confirm us as "better" somehow.

5. *Humans are rotten with perfection.*

The Duchess of Windsor once said, "You can never be too rich or too thin." Her statement illustrates not only two value hierarchies (thin/fat, rich/poor) but also Burke's idea that people feel compelled to pursue what they value, whether it is rational or not, self-destructive or not. You *can* be too thin — you can die from severe anorexia or malnutrition. Being rich has many problems too; you probably don't worry about your loved ones being kidnapped, but if you were extremely wealthy you would. Yet many people act as though when something is good, it is ultimately good and good in every degree. Attaching oneself to something — money, looks, education, sex, a political cause — in this unreasoning way determines how one acts, how one treats people, and how one spends one's time and money. This means that rhetoric—representations of reality that tie in to perceptions of value—can indeed compel behavior.

BURKE AND IDENTIFICATION

Burke's view of persuasion is very different from Aristotle's or other rationalistic models that see persuasion as a form of argument. In Burke's view, the fundamental element of persuasion is **identification**, the perceived sympathy, empathy, or analogy between speaker and audience (or reader and text, or listener and music, or viewer and movie, etc.—Burke includes literature and the arts in rhetoric). Burke thinks that as we listen to someone speak, we unconsciously gauge how similar that person is to us, in the sense that we are asking, "Does the world represented in this person's words seem to be *my* world also?" If the answer is yes, we identify with that speaker's rhetoric and with that speaker. To the extent that we accept that person's picture of the world, we'll also be moved to accept all the conclusions and implications that go with it.

For example, in Martin Luther King Jr.'s "I Have a Dream" speech, he portrayed the relationship between the civil rights movement and the symbolic meaning of being American. He could count on his audience to think that being a real American was a good thing, so he skillfully worked in symbols of "Americanness"—the Lincoln Memorial, "my country 'tis of thee," the landscape of the United States, the Constitution and Declaration of Independence, and so forth. King didn't so much *argue* that the civil rights movement was all-American as he *showed* that it was, by narrating an account of the meaning of America in which supporting civil rights is an inevitable consequence of being an American.

In contrast, Adolf Hitler used rhetoric in a similar way to a different end. To simplify a bit, during the 1930s Germans were upset that their economy was in ruins and that they had little political influence in Europe. Concerned that they had become a weak and powerless country, the public was ripe for a story in which they didn't turn out to be losers, but something else. In Hitler's telling, the Germans were not losers but victims—victims betrayed by the Jews. Of course, the story is wrong and absurd, but some Germans were motivated to believe it because it offered hope of dignity. Unfortunately, if they accepted the story, they accepted the implication that Jewish people were at fault and should be persecuted or punished. Hitler didn't have any evidence that Jews were at fault, just a convincing rhetorical story. Burke's theory of rhetoric explains how such stories are constructed and why people want to believe them.

Burke is important to modern rhetorical theory because he provided the first comprehensive theory that saw persuasion as more than rational argument plus emotion. Burke didn't offer a theory of argument, but an account of how people relate to language and to each other simultaneously. His theory seems better adapted than Aristotle's to our modern world teeming with media, saturated in public relations and "spin," and rife with nonlinguistic symbols.

Organization 5

In written texts, the organization of chapters and headings helps readers understand order and importance. Whether in a book where readers can flip back and forth or on a Web page where readers can scroll up and down, the information is arranged linearly (first, second, and so on). Readers can look in the index or table of contents, skip to a section and read it several times, or even start at the end, as with an exciting mystery story, and work backwards.

But speech is different. It happens in time and is fleeting; once words are spoken, they disappear into the air and aren't available for review. Audience members can't see a speech's structure in the way they can see a text's. Because of this, speakers work to indicate a speech's **organization** — the order in which things get said (also called *arrangement* or *disposition,* after the Latin *dispositio*) — to audiences. This strategy guides listeners through the speech and helps them identify and remember the most important points.

ORGANIZATIONAL PATTERNS

Organization orients listeners to a speech's structure by indicating what the arguments are and how they relate to one another. By distinguishing main points from subpoints, a speaker alerts the audience to what's most important in the speech. This makes the speech intelligible to the audience and helps them see where it is going, in terms of the goals of the speech and the means (arguments) for getting there.

How can you utilize organization? Let's start with the structure of speeches. Speeches naturally have a beginning, middle, and end, which speakers organize as the introduction, body, and conclusion. The speech's introduction sets the tone, letting the audience know what you will discuss and how it relates to them. The body of the speech presents your case, while the conclusion makes an appeal for action on the part of the audience. The body of your speech can be organized in different patterns to frame your argument, giving it shape and putting it into context.

Framing may be persuasive, because the order of the main points is important. While putting the strongest argument last is a common strategy (building toward your case), sometimes it's better to address a point right up front in order to dispel misunderstanding or counter a widely known objection to your thesis. Framing can also help adapt the arguments to the audience. For example, the issue of Social Security reform should be framed differently for younger and older audiences because the problem of having enough money in retirement affects each group differently; younger people will find points about the future the most powerful and salient, while older audiences will find arguments about current policy most important.

The body of a speech can be organized in several ways:

- *Topical.* This is the most common way to organize, by different topics — possibly in order of importance:

  My dad is a great guy because he is

  1. Generous to family and friends
  2. Good at his job
  3. Physically fit

- *Time.* This pattern organizes a speech chronologically:

  1. Before he graduated from medical school
  2. After graduation

  Or

  1. His college years
  2. His armed service years
  3. His entrepreneurship years

- *Places.* This pattern organizes a speech spatially:

  My dad is great

  1. At home
  2. In the office
  3. In the gym

- *Cause and effect.* This pattern first identifies causes and then explains effects:

  1. My dad's education
  2. What he's done with it

- *Problem/cause/solution.* This pattern first identifies a problem and then proposes a solution:

  1. The problem of deadbeat dads
  2. Causes of nonpayment of child support
  3. Solution: How to get them to support their kids

These patterns of organization provide a speaker with choices, depending on the audience and the subject, for organizing the subject matter. In most cases, the same body of information could be organized in several different ways. Speakers should choose a pattern that best suits the situation.

PARTS OF A SPEECH

While the basic structure of introduction-body-conclusion is fundamental to every speech, many variations have been proposed, differing mainly in the details. An elaborate and influential version can be found in the work of the Roman rhetoric teacher Quintilian (35 CE – ca. 100) in his *Traditions of Oratory,* where he defined the following parts of a speech (the italicized words are the Latin terms for these parts, some of which are still used today):

- *Exordium* ("commencement"). This is the introduction. Its purpose "is to prepare our audience in such a way that they will be disposed to lend a ready ear to the rest of our speech."[1] In other words, the introduction is functional, not just decorative. Speakers may use the introduction to allude to highly credible parties who are interested in the topic, and they may cultivate the appearance of their own neutrality and good sense about the issues at hand. Some speakers start with a joke to put the audience at ease, but most speakers use the introduction to acknowledge the important aspects of the setting and context.

- *Narratio* ("story," or backstory). This is the background information to a debate, policy, or issue; it sets the stage for the arguments to come. A citizen at a city council meeting, for example, might summarize the circumstances that led her to speak on a particular issue. In legal settings, the *narratio* outlines the facts of the case for those who don't already know them. Although there is no neutral way to do this, the speaker on each side will try to tell the story in a way that highlights the guilt or innocence of the accused.

- *Partitio* ("partition," or division of points). The division of points previews the speech's arguments. It builds on the *narratio,* or *backstory,* by pointing out how the speaker's case grows out of his version of events. The preview also orients the audience to the structure of the speech, helping them hear it more clearly.

- *Confirmatio* ("confirmation," or arguments). The body of the speech focuses on arguments that support the speaker's thesis. Here is where the speaker presents the best evidence he has and links it through careful argument to his thesis.

- *Refutatio* ("refutation"). In the course of a speech, it is often necessary to argue against some things; this is called counterargument. Sometimes it's necessary to discuss an entirely separate point to refute a specific argument; sometimes the refutations can be layered in along with the confirming arguments. When a speaker knows that there is an obvious objection to her argument, or that another speaker will raise one, then the speaker may need to challenge it, either denying it is valid altogether or arguing that it is irrelevant to her case.

- *Peroratio* ("conclusion"). The peroration (from the Latin *per* ["through"] + *oratio* ["speech"] meaning "to speak through to the end") involves both summing up and making a final plea to the audience for agreement. Typically, the peroration contains little or no new information; instead, it quickly reviews the arguments of the speech and why the audience should be persuaded by them. The conclusion also focuses on the connections to the audience that were established in the *exordium*, and it usually has a focus on *pathos*, the emotions of the listeners.

SAMPLE SPEECH

The sample speech "Water and You" illustrates how organization works. This speech concerns the problem of water pollution and is well adapted to its audience in southeastern Wisconsin; someone giving this speech in another part of the country would want to adapt it to the local water situation there. Also, the speaker's choice of "water recreation" as the way of adapting to the audience makes a general (and possibly boring) topic into a lively and personal one. The introduction establishes a vivid image of confronting the consequences of water pollution while framing the speech in terms of the audience's interest in water recreation. For another audience, the speaker might have framed the speech in terms of harm to the recreation industry or to small towns.

The organizational pattern is problem/cause/solution, which makes sense given the speaker's goal of getting people to change their water use habits. For the problem point, the speaker chose to organize spatially, moving from city pollution to state pollution. He could have organized topically, by dividing the point into lakes versus rivers, or natural versus artificial pollution. The cause point is organized topically, according to sources of pollution; it could also have been organized chronologically, exploring older and newer sources of pollution to emphasize how the current audience is involved—that is, pollution is still happening, not just left over from a previous generation. The solutions are also organized topically, explaining what the audience can do and what the government can do; they could also have been organized spatially (according to regions of the state) or chronologically (present and future).

Water and You[2]

Imagine a beautiful summer's day; you've gone out to a lake, and you're enjoying a swim in the warm water. You splash around with your friends, reveling in the day. You dive under water for a moment, and when you come up, you are face-to-face with a dead fish. Its cold eye seems to be staring right at you, almost accusing you. Of course, fish die every day, that's part of life. But more and more freshwater species are dying at   *Exordium*

an ever-faster rate, and it's due to the pollution of the water
supply.

We have to face the fact that we may often be swimming in   *Narratio*
sewage, chemicals, dead fish and more. We have become aware
over the last forty years that pollution is a fact of modern life,
and when we ignore it, we always pay the price. There are many
kinds of pollution: air, soil, water. But because water is such a
precious resource and we take it for granted, it is an especially
important one.

Our water supply is being destroyed today due to all the   *Thesis*
pollution that contaminates our water, and if it continues we
may be finding more and more dead fish on every shore.

I'd like to explain how water pollution is ruining the recre-   *Division of*
ational use of water, and then show you how our daily water   *Points*
usage is a major factor in increasing pollution, and, finally, how
we can all make changes that will ensure clean water in the
future.

First, pollution is eating into our recreational water   *Confirmatio 1:*
activities. Here in Milwaukee we can't be blind to the effects   *The problem of*
of pollution on our lives. In warm weather, many of us flock   *pollution*
to Lake Michigan or one of the thousands of lakes scattered
throughout Wisconsin. In winter, ice-fishing remains a phenome-
nally popular sport. People swim, boat, and fish throughout
Wisconsin, but the more polluted our waters get, the less
appetizing it becomes.

In the Milwaukee area, 84% of our water comes from Lake
Michigan. For the decade ending in 2003 alone, the total sewage
dumped into Lake Michigan is as much as 22 billion gallons!
(http://www.greatlakesdirectory.org/wi/070203_great_lakes.htm)
While the Deep Tunnel Project was supposed to solve the sewage
problem, it hasn't — we're just using too much water. The
amount of mercury in Great Lakes fish is high enough that preg-
nant women and nursing mothers are advised not to eat fish
caught there. My neighbor is a water scientist who studies Lake
Michigan; not only won't she eat lake fish while she's nursing,
she told me she wouldn't let her son eat lake fish until he is at
least five years old.

And it's not just Lake Michigan. "The DNR's fish advisory for
mercury contamination stands at 321 lakes and river segments
and includes many favorite Wisconsin fishing waters such as
Lake Wissota, Tomahawk Lake, Trout Lake, Lake Monona, and
segments of the Wisconsin, Wolf, Black, and St. Croix rivers.
Most lakes in the state have yet to be tested, but so far roughly
one out of every three has had some fish — most often walleyes —

with unsafe mercury levels." (Wisconsin Stewardship Network, http://www.wsn.org/energy/mercury.html)

According to the Groundwater Foundation, the average American uses 100 gallons a day, and that's a lot of water, especially since about 50% of Americans get their water from groundwater sources — water lying underground in the water table, not aboveground in lakes and rivers. Groundwater gets contaminated when products we use every day, such as gasoline, oil, road salts, and chemicals, seep into the groundwater and pollute it, potentially making it unfit for human use. Where do these contaminants come from? In many cases, industrial sites such as storage tanks, hazardous waste sites, and landfills. In other cases, it's the widespread use of road salts and agricultural chemicals such as fertilizers and pesticides. Anyone who depends on the roads in winter or eats from these farms is participating, personally, in polluting the waters. In addition, septic systems and municipal treatment plants deliberately or inadvertently dump water laced with sewage, chemicals, and drugs into the ground. Yes — drugs! People excrete whatever their bodies don't metabolize, and so everything from ibuprofen to estrogen ends up in the water supply.

Confirmatio 2: The causes of pollution

Now, how is our own personal water use involved in all this pollution? The more we use, the more groundwater sources are depleted, and the harder it is for natural filtering processes to clean the water underground. The more we use, the more water municipal plants have to clean, and the overflow into the lake is that much more likely.

So while it's important to limit industrial and agricultural sources of pollution, it's also important, even though we live near the fifth-largest freshwater lake in the world, to conserve the water we use, and to avoid polluting the lakes and groundwater.

Confirmatio 3: The Solution

It's actually pretty easy to do, since we tend not to think much about our water use.

There are some things that everyone can easily do: Take shorter showers, avoid baths, do fewer loads of laundry by making sure you only do it when you have a full load. Don't run the water while you brush — you're not using it, and you'd be surprised how quickly it adds up. Don't flush pills or medicine down the toilet; take them to a site in your city for proper disposal.

Avoid using fertilizers or pesticides in your yard, since the chemicals wash down the drains or straight into the ground. If you wash your car, use a natural soap, such as castile soap, that won't pollute when it goes down the drain.

The state and federal government must do their parts,
certainly, by mandating cleanup of waste sites and controlling
industrial and agricultural runoff. But everyone has a part, and
we have to do ours.

We don't need to run out of clean water. Through everyday   *Conclusion*
actions, we can reduce the stress on the system, make more
water available, and reduce how much we pollute.

Boating, fishing, swimming — these are part of our way of   *Peroratio*
life. We don't need to give them up. Nobody wants to face the
dead accusing eye of fish, and we don't have to. We can simply
make the difference.

6 Style

"Words," said Cicero, "are the dress of thought." What did he mean? Think of it this way: you don't go out of the house naked, but you choose what to wear. Well, your ideas don't just leave your head "naked" by themselves, but you choose words for them. Like your wardrobe, you have a choice about the words you use. They can be plain or fancy, cheap or expensive, sexy or boring; they can show off your deepest thoughts or hide them. Just as there is no neutral way to dress (after all, anything you put on is a choice that says something about you), there is no neutral way of choosing words when speaking. In this chapter, we're going to look at two ways that speakers can "dress up" their arguments. First, we'll talk about **figures**, which are creative arrangements of words in phrases or sentences that catch the audience's attention and focus it on your key ideas. Then we'll talk about tropes, which involve replacing words or phrases with less literal terms to embellish your rhetorical language.

FIGURES

Figures apply to phrases. People speak (more or less) in sentences composed of words and phrases, and sometimes rearranging the structure of words and phrases makes them more effective. An effective phrase in speaking is like an effective melody in music; it should have a shape, be appealing, and be memorable—something you can hum. The major factor in making a phrase memorable is novelty. The expressions we create for speeches need to be different from our ordinary speech—they need to be more structured and focused and thus stand out more. Let's look at some of the main verbal figures.

ANTITHESIS

Antithesis means "putting opposites together." This can occur in a sentence with two parts, where there is contrast or opposition between the first part and the second. For example:

> One small step for a man; one giant leap for mankind.
> —*Neil Armstrong/James Dickey*

Aristotle claimed that "popularity of style is mainly due to antitheses,"[1] and such juxtapositions are indeed impressive and memorable. Antithesis helps an audience follow a speech by highlighting the contrast between important ideas. Consider this example from Richard Nixon's 1969 eulogy for Senator Everett Dirksen:

A politician knows that more important than the bill that is proposed is the law that is passed. A politician knows that his friends are not always his allies, and that his adversaries are not his enemies. A politician knows how to make the process of democracy work and loves the intricate workings of the democratic system. A politician knows not only how to count votes but how to make his vote _____.[2]   —*Richard Nixon*

You can easily guess the last word of this passage (*count*), if you were following the structure of the sentences by listening or reading closely. There are different ways to create the opposition in an antithesis:

- *Plain double antithesis:* In this type of figure, the contrast can be between individual words or between phrases.

   If a free society cannot help the *many* who are *poor,* it cannot save the *few* who are *rich.*   —*John F. Kennedy*

   Not a *victory of a party,* but a *celebration of freedom.*   —*John F. Kennedy*

   The rights of man come not from the *generosity of the state* but from the *hand of God.*   —*John F. Kennedy*

   Our *first* kiss was so *sweet,* but our *final* goodbye was so *bitter.*

- *Double-reverse antithesis,* or *chiasmus:* In this figure, which is similar to antithesis, the opposition is in the reversed order of key words, which creates the opposite meaning.

   Let us never *negotiate* out of *fear,* but let us never *fear* to *negotiate.*
                                                                  —*John F. Kennedy*

   You can take the *boy* out of the *country,* but you can't take the *country* out of the *boy.*

Antitheses are especially useful in a peroration, or conclusion (see Chapter 5), to make a point memorable.

REPETITION

Even though people commonly repeat many words in ordinary conversation, structured repetition is generally avoided. Yet in a speech, such repetition can add emphasis and make a point more memorable. Although it's hard to say exactly why repetition is captivating, the first century BCE Roman rhetoric textbook *Rhetorica Ad Herrenium* noted, "In the four kinds of figures [of repetition] which I have thus far set forth, the frequent recourse to the same word is not dictated by verbal poverty; rather there inheres in the repetition an elegance which the ear can distinguish more easily than words can explain."[3] In other words, listeners will like repetition even if they don't know why. Repetition of words, phrases, or sounds (rhyme, alliteration, and assonance) can occur at the beginning, middle, or end of successive clauses, sentences, sections, or even whole speeches. Different combinations produce different forms of repetition.

Repetition of Words and Phrases

- **Anaphora**, a Greek word meaning "repetition," is the common term for the repeated beginnings of successive words or phrases:

   > [W]e *shall* not flag or fail. *We shall* go on to the end, *we shall* fight in France, *we shall* fight on the seas and oceans, *we shall* fight with growing confidence and growing strength in the air, *we shall* defend our Island, whatever the cost may be, *we shall* fight on the beaches, *we shall* fight on the landing grounds, *we shall* fight in the fields and in the streets, *we shall* fight in the hills; *we shall* never surrender. —*Winston Churchill*

- **Antistrophe** repeats the endings of successive phrases:

   > A government of *the people,* by *the people,* and for *the people.*
   > —*Abraham Lincoln*

- **Interlacement** combines the above two figures (anaphora and antistrophe) by repeating words at both the beginning and the ending of sentences:

   > *Who are they* who have often broken treaties? *The Carthaginians. Who are they* who have waged war with severest cruelty? *The Carthaginians. Who are they* who have blemished the face of Italy? *The Carthaginians. Who are they* who now ask for pardon? *The Carthaginians.* See then how appropriate it is to let their request be granted. —*Ad Herrenium*

- **Anadiplosis** is the doubling or repetition of a word in the last clause of one sentence and in the first clause of the next. This connects the two thoughts and emphasizes a particular concept.

   > And so even though we face the difficulties of today and tomorrow, I still have a *dream.* It is a *dream* deeply rooted in the American *dream.*
   > —*Martin Luther King Jr.*

Repetition of Sounds

Repetition can also occur with sounds.

- **Alliteration** is the repetition of the initial sounds of words:

   > Peter Piper picked a peck of pickled peppers . . .

- **Rhyme** is the repetition of final sounds:

   > If my mind can conceive it, and my heart can believe it, I know I can achieve it.
   > —*Jesse Jackson*

- **Assonance** is the repetition of the middle sounds:

  > How much wood would a wood chuck chuck if a wood chuck could chuck wood? A wood chuck would chuck all the wood he could chuck, if a wood chuck could chuck wood.

The advantage of repetition is that it makes a speaker's main ideas especially memorable and gives them added emotional force.

PROGRESSION (KLIMAX)

Klimax is a Greek word meaning "ladder," and the effect of the klimax is like the progression, in steps, up a ladder. Such progression adds direction to repetition because the repeated elements create a sense of movement:

> He who controls Berlin, controls Germany,
>   and he who controls Germany, controls Europe,
>   and he who controls Europe, controls the world.

The layering of ideas and images makes the logic expressed here particularly memorable.

The best strategy for progression is to leave the most important item until the end, building up to the point you want the audience to remember:

> All this will not be finished in the first one hundred days. Nor will it be finished in the first one thousand days, nor in the life of this administration, nor perhaps in our lifetime on this planet.   —*John F. Kennedy*

Here is an example from the Bible that combines anadiplosis and klimax:

> But we glory also in tribulations, knowing that tribulation worketh patience; and patience trial; and trial hope; and hope confoundeth not.
>   —*St. Paul, Rom. 5:3–5*

OTHER FIGURES

Here is a sample listing of other useful figures.

- **Asyndeton** involves omitting conjunctions or other connections, speeding a sentence up and placing emphasis on the clauses or verbs themselves:

  > I came, I saw, I conquered. (*Veni, vedi, vici.*)   —*Julius Caesar*

  > With this faith, we will be able to work together, to pray together, to struggle together, to go to jail together, to stand up for freedom together, knowing that we will be free one day.   —*Martin Luther King Jr.*

  > On life's journey faith is nourishment, virtuous deeds are a shelter, wisdom is the light by day, right mindfulness is the protection by night.   —*Buddha*

- A **rhetorical question** is one that doesn't expect a literal answer. Instead, it either invites the audience to fill in an obvious answer ("Who else could have done the crime?") or provokes thought, as in this example:

  > If I am not for myself, then who will be for me? And if I am only for myself, then what am I? And if not now, when?   — *Rabbi Hillel*

- **Tricolon** is a grouping of three clauses that can be understood as a series of individual examples or related ideas. (If there are only two clauses, the listener may only compare or contrast the ideas instead of seeing them as a series.)

  > Tell me and I forget. Teach me and I remember. Involve me and I learn.
  > —*Benjamin Franklin*

Some figures are equally appropriate in speech and writing; others, such as asyndeton, are more appropriate to speech. No matter what figures you use, it takes a little bit of courage to depart from ordinary diction and use the structure of language to call attention to and reinforce ideas—but the effect can be well worth the effort.

TROPES

Here is something interesting to think about: there are more objects, events, and situations in the world than there are words to describe them. Hypothetically, it would be impossible for a language to have a unique word for every phenomenon that one might encounter. Such a language would be far too tough to learn, and the dictionary would take up a massive library! One thing that makes language a shared cultural enterprise is that certain words work in a number of different contexts, and people can adapt the meaning of older words to accommodate new situations.

In everyday life, whether in speaking or writing, we often stumble upon objects, events, or situations that we don't have precisely the right words for. How do speakers or writers cope with this? One strategy is to borrow a word or idea from another context and use that to talk about the new phenomenon. For example, when the Internet first took off, there wasn't a particularly good word to describe what people did online. It was a little bulky to say that they were "browsing from Web page to Web page by following links," so a new word usage was born: people said they were "surfing the net." No one actually thought that looking at the Web involved the ocean or a surf board, but the connection between looking at the Internet and surfing made some sense: it captured the idea of being taken up by a wave of information and being directed by its flow. This idea of "surfing" the net is a **trope**—a substitution of a word or phrase by a less literal word or phrase.

The term *trope* comes from the Greek term *tropos,* meaning "turn," "way," "manner," or "style." This root definition underlies the familiar comment that someone has "turned a good phrase," meaning that he has a persuasive or beautiful style of speaking. Tropes are key building blocks of rhetorical style because they allow a speaker to substitute indirect or less literal words for direct or more literal ones. Such substitutions are especially helpful when it is difficult to convey an idea directly, when a speaker wants to amplify a point, or when a straightforward phrase doesn't convey the full force of an idea. For example, on a hot day you might say, "It's an oven outside." The idea of the oven vividly substitutes for the more direct or literal description, "It's very hot outside."

How are tropes different from figures? One view is that tropes, unlike figures, invoke images by moving beyond simple reference or description. Think about a contrast between the most straightforward and literal functions of language and more rhetorical language. For an example of straightforward language, consider the simple descriptive sentence: "The book is on the table." Each word in this sentence has a literal meaning: the two nouns refer to objects, and the way that they (as well as the article *the* and the preposition *on*) refer to objects is direct and unadorned. The word *book* refers to printed pages bound together, *is on* refers to the book's location, and *table* refers to the piece of furniture that keeps the book from falling to the ground. For an example of rhetorical language, consider the sentence "The fever is on the rise." Although this sentence can have a literal meaning if it refers to an ill person's temperature, it can take on rhetorical meaning if, say, it refers to a revolutionary movement or a groundswell of excitement.

There are several types of tropes, and we will look at a few examples here.

METONYMY

Metonymy is a trope that replaces literal meaning with another meaning commonly associated with an object, word, or concept. Think of metonymy as borrowing a concept or quality from a word's or phrase's natural context. For example, people often refer to everything in the news media as "the press." Originally, this terminology made literal sense because the main way of getting news was through the newspaper, and newspapers are printed on printing presses. Nowadays, we get much of our news through other sources, yet we still understand what it means to talk about "the press." Metonymy enables us to use something commonly associated with the news (the printing press) as a term referring to all possible forms of news media (television, radio, magazines, the Internet). The idea of "the press" works—even when we aren't literally referring to a printing press—because of the association between presses and the media.

Metonymy enriches our language choices by allowing us to say things in compact, elegant, and artistic ways. Which sounds better: "He's a fast driver who's always pushing the gas pedal" or "She has a lead foot"? The associations between lead and weight, and between weight and depressing the gas pedal, provide a compact and rich image that helps us visualize a fast driver. Indeed, language has so many possibilities for association that we aren't always conscious of all the ways that it can be playful or interesting. The fact that we are not always conscious of these associations is not a bad thing at all. Rather, this depth and richness allow skilled speakers to pull out interesting, beautiful, or playful meanings from the field of words, and thus to continually surprise and delight listeners.

SYNECDOCHE

Metonymy is closely related to **synecdoche**, which is the substitution of a part of something for its whole, or the whole of something for its part. For example, you might have heard someone say she works because she has "mouths to feed." While it is true that people do use their mouths to eat, technically one does not feed a mouth alone; one feeds a person who has a mouth. In this instance, the synecdoche works because the word *mouths* (the part) stands in for the actual people (the whole).

Synecdoche can also work by taking the whole of something as a stand-in for a specific part. For example, imagine you get a parking ticket from a campus police officer. Even though it was an individual officer who wrote the ticket, in grumbling to your friends you might say something like "I can't believe the university [or the campus police] is so strict about parking." In this instance, the whole (either the university or the campus police) stands in for the part (the individual officer who wrote the ticket).

The interesting thing about synecdoche is that we use it so often we don't even realize it. Think about commonly used phrases that substitute a part for the whole, like *all hands on deck* (viewing the specific sailor as defined by his hands) or specific product names for a whole class of goods, as in *Xerox* for all photocopiers or *Kleenex* for all tissues. There are also very commonly used substitutions of the whole for the part, as when people say that the government, the administration, or the White House speaks or has an opinion (substituting the whole institution for a person or group of people within that institution).

METAPHOR

Perhaps the most well known trope is *metaphor.* The term *metaphor* comes from the Greek words *meta,* meaning "beyond," "above," or "change," and *pherein,* meaning "to carry" or "bear." A **metaphor** carries or bears another meaning beyond its literal one. You may have already learned about metaphors by comparing them with similes. A simile makes a comparison by noting that one thing is "like," "as" or "resembles" another thing: a runner is as "fast as a bullet," or angry eyes are "like lasers." While a simile (in actuality, a special kind of analogy) *associates* one thing with another thing, a metaphor actually says that one thing *is* another thing. A famous line from Shakespeare's *As You Like It*, "all the world's a stage," is a metaphor. To say "all the world is like a stage" would be to use a simile (and make an analogy).

Metaphors import the qualities of one word or idea to elaborate on the qualities of another. For instance, we might say that a successful idea or enterprise "takes flight." We do not mean that the idea or enterprise is literally flying, but that it has the qualities of "taking off" in that it is soaring to meet its potential. Anyone who has thought long, hard, and creatively about a problem has had the experience of thought "taking off," which is partly why the metaphor works so well.

Sometimes, though, it's necessary to borrow words — or, more specifically, metaphors — that are less naturally connected to a given context. For example, when people needed to coin a term that referred to the start of a mountain range, they said that they were at the "foot of a mountain." In instances like this, metaphors take on a special form: **catachresis**, which is classically defined as a harsh or "abusive" metaphor. The harshness or abusiveness is not a quality of the content of the catachresis, but instead refers to the fact that it seems a bit of a stretch or strain from the truth, and thus it is "harsh or abusive" on the listener's ear. In some ways, the difference between metaphor and catachresis is in the eye (ear?) of the beholder — one person's metaphor is another person's catachresis. But in some cases the metaphor, though useful, really is somewhat strained. After all, we don't say that we are at the legs or the neck of a mountain. Although the association of feet in "foot of the mountain" is close enough to be a workable metaphor, it is also enough of a stretch that many rhetoricians consider it a catachresis.

WHY TROPES MATTER

For a long time, many rhetoricians were suspicious of tropes, seeing them as only pretty ornamentation for language. In fact, some schools of rhetoric (for instance, that of Ramus, mentioned in Chapter 1) thought that tropes were outright dangerous because they got in the way of clear and direct expression. This line of thought saw rhetoric as a way of presenting an argument or as a way of exerting an effect on an audience. In this tradition, the core concern of rhetoric is Aristotle's *logos* — the logic of a point (see Chapter 4). If you are a firm believer that *logos* is at the heart of rhetoric, you might think either that tropes are only ornaments that dress up a point, or, worse yet, that they actively detract from logic.

However, other thinkers (including Kenneth Burke, mentioned in Chapter 4) thought that tropes were at the core of rhetoric. In this view, the goals of rhetoric are to understand the ways that people play with language and to think about how claims might be made most persuasively. This model sees tropes as one of the best manifestations of the fact that no language is neutral or unadorned — everything that is said or written is dependent on multiple meanings, play, and artifice used to persuade people.

Yet tropes can do more than illustrate that all language is dependent on artifice. You can use tropes to understand not only texts but also social investments, or ways of thinking about identity. Consider the discussion in Chapter 2 about the second persona and publics. One of the main points was that publics and audiences do not exist in advance but are evoked by speakers' language. One example was the phrase "we the people" in the preamble to the U.S. Constitution. The idea "we the people" is also a trope — specifically, metonymy. This example of metonymy is linked to the concept of "public" that the founding fathers hoped to evoke.

Of course, one could do the same thing with synecdoche or metaphor. For instance, an attack on specific Americans is often connected via synecdoche with an attack on all Americans. When the Japanese attacked Pearl Harbor in World War II, people did not say, "This was a terrible attack on Hawaii and the U.S. naval base there." Instead, people spoke about it as an attack on America. The part (a naval base in Hawaii) was defined through the lens of the whole (America).

In the same way tropes of identity such as "Americanness" can function metaphorically and provide a new way of understanding and relating to events. For example, after the 9/11 attacks, the September 12 issue of the French newspaper *Le Monde* contained an article that famously declared, "We are all Americans today." This is a metaphor. The French citizen who wrote it was not an American, nor was he or she simply saying that the French are like Americans (in that they are also subject to terrorist attacks). Instead, "We are all Americans today" meant that the outpouring of sympathy and solidarity after 9/11 made people metaphorically identify with Americans.

Figures and tropes demonstrate that language is persuasive in part because it can bend and accommodate to make new, creative, and inventive meanings. Indeed, a full definition of rhetoric must acknowledge the ways that figures and tropes persuade — not simply by providing pretty or ornate language, but by bringing to bear associations that make words convincing — argumentatively, emotionally, and aesthetically.

Rhetoric in Contemporary Life 7

This *Essential Guide to Rhetoric* has a fairly classical focus, and it would be natural to ask how these materials, some of them 2,500 years old, are relevant to today's world. This question is an important one, and there are several answers to it. We can connect rhetorical theory to modern public speaking and public communication, to online forms of communication, and to hopes for an engaged political life.

RHETORIC AND PUBLIC SPEAKING

In the twenty-first century, we're increasingly aware of communication in its many forms. Mass communication includes everything from TV and cable to news Web sites and all the content—textual, audio, and video—available for downloading from the Internet. Oral communication includes everything we engage in and produce: conversing in person with friends or family; e-mailing coworkers; using Facebook, MySpace, or instant messaging; and much more. Each of these forms of communication is meaningful, not only because of who we are communicating with but also because of how we communicate. In a world full of communication technology, you may wonder whether public speaking matters at all. Why is it worthwhile to learn how to stand up and speak in front of a group? Why is it worthwhile to learn how to listen?

Public speaking is a worthwhile study for many reasons. First, and most important, despite the diversity of forms of communication, a similar logic governs them all. Good public speakers know how to choose goals and adapt messages to their audiences by crafting responsible and effective appeals. Once you understand these principles, you will find them useful in many other contexts. So, whether meeting someone in person or posting a profile on MySpace, similar principles will guide the choices you make.

Second, despite modern communication technology, public speaking is still part of everyday life. Certainly, the workplace demands it; high-quality presentations are required in virtually every profession. Beyond the workplace, speaking in person is a relatively common occurrence. If you want to communicate with your city council, you can post a message to the city Web site, but for maximum effect, showing up and speaking are best. Many organizations do much of their business face to face—community boards, nonprofits, school boards, and so on.

Third, the tradition of public speaking focuses on the civic context, which matters more than ever today. Citizens in a democracy need to be able to speak as citizens to fellow citizens. Speakers approach public speaking as civic when they appeal to audience members as equals in the spirit of reasoned, joint decision-making. This democratic context is fundamental to public speaking. Public speaking isn't advertising, marketing, or sales (though sometimes speakers do all those things). Needless to say, this approach can be useful in business and professional contexts, but it remains an essential part of public life.

RHETORIC AND ONLINE COMMUNICATION

Do the principles of classical rhetoric apply to electronic communication? Absolutely.[1] Two main areas are especially relevant: ethos and organization.

ETHOS AND ONLINE PRESENTATION

Consider the concept of ethos, or the character of the speaker. As we discussed in Chapter 4, much of speakers' ethos is constructed through what they choose to say and how they choose to say it. This principle is just as applicable to online and print environments as it is to public speaking. Imagine two different students (Jones and Smith) sending an e-mail to an instructor:

> From: jones@university.edu
>   To: Prof@university.edu
>
> y did u grade my test so hard
> i should get a better grade

and

> From: smith@university.edu
>   To: Prof@university.edu
>
> Dear Professor:
>
> I've been working hard in your course all term, and I've found it challenging and rewarding. I was disappointed in my last exam grade, and I'd like to talk it over with you, since I think the grade doesn't reflect my knowledge or my actual performance on the exam. Let's meet at your convenience to discuss it.
>
> Thank you,
> S. Smith

Jones and Smith present themselves as very different students. Jones, with lazy text-message spelling, no punctuation, and scant indication of what she wants, doesn't come across as a very serious student, and you can imagine the professor wondering if he should take her seriously. Conversely, Smith uses full sentences and standard spelling and punctuation, marking her as a more serious student (after all, good writing skills are one of the things students learn in college). What's more, she makes clear her relationship to the course and the nature of her concerns about her grade. Her presentation is honest and sincere. Smith may have felt angry when she received her grade, just as Jones did, but she is able to put that aside and deal with the issue professionally — that is her ethos. Even when the medium is e-mail, the same rhetorical proofs apply.

ONLINE ORGANIZATION

Consider also the organization of Web sites. These pages have layers and hypertext, and they are not strictly linear like a speech or a book. But the same principles of organization still apply. For example, on the homepage there should be an introduction to the site and an explanation of why someone might use it. Typically, a set of links at the top of the page alerts the reader to the structure of the site as a whole, just as the preview to a speech does, and a link to a "site map" gives an overview of the site. Just as there are transitions between points in a speech, there are labeled links that guide the user through the site.

When designing a Web site, the developer thinks about its structure in the same way that a speaker makes choices about the body of a speech: How many major sections? In what order? What's the most important aspect, and how should it be highlighted? For example, if a Web site concerns the rating of political candidates, the site could sort by candidate ("Find the candidate you are interested in.") or rating ("Look at the highest- and lowest-ranked candidates."). The developer may let users choose or may make the decision to use only one; either way, it is a decision about organization.

These are just two examples of how classical principles of rhetoric apply to electronic media communication. If you think about the organizing principles of a television news program, or the structure of a MySpace page, or the way the letters to a newspaper's editorial page are written, you can see the application of classical rhetoric to almost any context of communication.

RHETORIC AND REASONABLE POLITICS

One of the debates about rhetoric in antiquity was whether it was good or bad for the political system. On one side were those, like Plato, who were convinced that rhetoric was superficial, and that people were so easily misled by it that neither the public nor rhetoric could be trusted. On the other side were those, like Aristotle, who thought that rhetoric, at its best, could be a system of reasoned decision-making that was necessary for any form of democracy. He was not naïve to rhetoric's darker side, however. Commenting on the unethical practices he saw in court (making jurors angry or sympathetic when it wasn't relevant to the case at hand), he said, "[It] is wrong to warp the jury by leading them into anger, or envy or pity; that is the same as if someone made a straightedge rule crooked before using it."[2] Aristotle's point is that for a group of people—a jury or a voting public—to come to a reasonable and just decision, speakers have to provide the kind of arguments and evidence that will allow them to do so. If someone is on trial for stealing, working the jury into a lather about the basic unfairness of society doesn't get to the point of making a good decision about guilt or innocence.

We face the same problems today. Surrounded by the mass media, we have more political discourse available to us than ever before, but we still wonder whether it is helping or hurting the political process. Ideally, in a democracy, arguments circulate through the public, and people make up their minds about candidates, laws, and policies based on evidence. The key term here is *ideally*. In practice, it only sometimes works out that way.[3] Often it doesn't. Based on those perceived failures, some people are ready to give up on democratic discourse in general. But the classical tradition of rhetoric, born to serve the first democracy in ancient Athens, offers tools for thinking that might make it work after all. In this sense, the classical tradition is *normative* rather than *descriptive*; it focuses on how we ought to communicate (at our best) rather than how we do communicate (at our worst).

The rhetorical tradition teaches us how to become articulate citizens, worthy participants in a shared system of government. The tools and concepts outlined in this book constitute a system for becoming a democratic speaker, someone who can ethically take into account audiences and publics in the context of well-supported and clear arguments for any given position. Although rhetoric can also reveal how deception and dishonesty in political communication work, its more important function is to explain how we can do better, how we can create the best system of government—and the best country—possible.

GLOSSARY

adaptation   A principle by which speakers try to connect their audiences or public to what they are saying by developing arguments that relate to audience members' knowledge and experience.

address   The formal term for a relationship between a speaker or sender and an audience or receiver; a way of saying that a speaker and an audience have a relationship whereby each understands what the other is doing.

alliteration   When successive words begin with the same sound.

amphiboly   A term meaning that grammar can be ambiguous.

anadiplosis   The doubling or repetition of a word in the last clause of one sentence and in the first clause of the next.

anaphora   A Greek term meaning "repetition"; the common term for the repeated beginnings of successive words or phrases.

antistrophe   A figure that repeats the endings of successive phrases.

antithesis   In a sentence with two parts, a contrast or opposition between the first part and the second part.

appropriateness   Suitability or compatibility; in rhetorical communication, it is whether a speaker's tone, word choices, and delivery match the situation.

Aristotle's types of speeches   Aristotle classified different kinds of speech by their purposes: forensic (for use at a trial), epideictic (for use at a funeral), and deliberative (for use in the senate).

assonance   When successive words have the same sound in the middle.

asyndeton   The omission of conjunctions or other connections, speeding a sentence up and placing emphasis on the clauses or verbs.

audience   The group of people to whom a symbol, speech, or message is directed; the group of people who need to be persuaded to take action.

burden of proof   The principle by which accusers must prove that the accused is guilty, but the accused does not have to prove that he or she is innocent.

catechresis   The inappropriate use of a word for the effect of surprise ("He downloaded the music sight unseen").

clash   A collision or conflict; in rhetorical communication, when two arguments meet head-on over an issue, they clash.

confirmatio   The body of a speech, in which the speaker presents the best evidence and links it through careful argument to the thesis.

constraints   The things that stand in the way of dealing with the exigence. See also *exigence.*

contingent   Dependent on; in rhetorical communication, the outcome of a rhetorical act is contingent on audience reaction.

deliberative speech   A speech that argues for a course of future action. See also *Aristotle's types of speeches.*

discourse   Any speech, written or spoken, as well as the exchange of symbols or meanings in any context: books, newspapers, pictures, movies, Web sites, music, and so on.

enthymemes Legitimately persuasive arguments that are not formally valid.

epideictic speech A speech used more at an event (such as a funeral) than at a specific institution (such as in court), also called an occasional speech. See also *Aristotle's types of speeches.*

ethos A speaker's credibility (believability) and trustworthiness.

example A kind of rhetorical argument that speakers use to prove their claims inductively.

exigence The problem or occasion for change that causes someone to speak.

exordium The introduction of a speech.

fallacies Mistakes and errors in argumentation and reasoning that make an argument invalid.

figures Interesting arrangements of words in phrases or sentences that catch the audience's attention and focus it on key ideas.

forensic speech A legal speech. See also *Aristotle's types of speeches.*

genre A type of speech; the idea that different types of speeches work better in different situations.

identification The perceived sympathy, empathy, or analogy between speaker and audience.

inductive reasoning A type of reasoning that assumes that if something is true in specific cases, then it is true in general.

informational speaking A way of speaking that seeks to help an audience understand information, often for a purpose.

interlacement The combination of anaphora and antistrophe by repeating words at both the beginning and the ending of sentences. See also *anaphora; antistrophe.*

issue Any point on which people could take different sides.

kairos The right time to deliver a message to an audience in order to persuade them.

klimax A Greek word meaning "ladder," the effect of which is like the progression, in steps, up a ladder; in this type of figure, repeated elements create a sense of movement.

logos The logic of a speech; the arguments that it makes.

medium The means of transmitting information between sender and receiver.

message The content that someone or something seeks to convey.

metaphor When a word is used in a nonliteral, but meaningful, sense.

metonymy When a whole is referred to by a part ("all hands on deck") or by an attribute ("put some sweat into it").

narratio The background information to a debate, policy, or issue; it sets the stage for the arguments to come.

occasional speech See *epideictic speech.*

organization The order in which things get said to an audience; a means of orienting listeners to a speech's structure by indicating what the arguments are and how they relate to one another.

partitio The division of points in which the speaker previews the arguments to be made in a speech.

pathos The emotional state of the audience, as produced by the speaker or speech.

peroratio Conclusion; the part of a speech in which the speaker sums up and makes a final plea to the audience for agreement.

persuasion The act of convincing someone of something.

persuasive speaking A way of speaking that seeks to cause a change in the audience.

polysemy A term meaning that words can have multiple meanings.

premises Propositions or statements.

presumption A tie-breaking principle; a prior decision about which side should be given the benefit of the doubt in the case of a tie.

proofs The ways of making speech persuasive. See also *ethos; logos; pathos.*

public The commonality among people that is based on consumption of common texts (shared experience in society).

public sphere A place common to all, where ideas and information are explored.

receiver Someone, something, or some group that receives a message.

refutatio Counterargument; the part of a speech during which the speaker refutes other arguments.

rhetoric The study of producing discourses and interpreting how, when, and why discourses are persuasive.

rhetorical criticism The act of reading an object (a speech or a text) in the light of its surroundings.

rhetorical question A question that does not expect a literal answer, but either invites the audience to fill in an obvious answer or provokes thought.

rhetorical situation The context, time, audience, and circumstances that surround a speech.

rhyme When successive words end with the same sound.

second persona A term used by modern rhetorician Edwin Black to describe the persona of the audience, which is created in response to (or evoked by) the speaker.

sender Someone or something that sends a message.

speaking to entertain A way of speaking that is often ceremonial and seeks to please or amuse an audience.

status quo The current state of affairs; literally, "what stands (now)."

stock issues Issues of an argument that are known in advance because they are standardized issues in a given context.

strategic Important for carrying out a plan; in rhetorical communication, a speaker plans how to frame the message in order to persuade the audience.

syllogisms Arguments in which two true premises (propositions or statements) validly imply a third statement, the conclusion of the argument.

synecdoche The type of metonymy focusing on the part-whole relationship.

techne An art or technique.

topoi The general forms that arguments take, regardless of their actual content.

tricolon A grouping of three clauses that can be understood as a series of individual examples or related ideas.

trope A figure of speech using less literal or direct words or phrases.

 **NOTES**

CHAPTER 1

1. *The American Heritage Dictionary of the English Language,* 4th ed., s.v. "Rhetoric," http://www.bartleby.com/61/80/R0218000.html (accessed April 25, 2007).
2. Aristotle *Rhetoric,* 1.2.1355b.

CHAPTER 2

1. Gorgias, "Encomium of Helen," Rosamond Kent Sprague, ed. *The Older Sophists: A Complete Translation by Several Hands of the Fragments in Die Fragmente Der Vorsokraticker,* ed. Diels-Kranz with a New Edition of Antiphon and of Euthydemus (Columbia, SC: University of South Carolina Press, 1972), 50–54.
2. Edwin Black, "The Second Persona." *The Quarterly Journal of Speech* 55 (1970): 113.
3. John Dewey, *The Public and Its Problems* (Athens, OH: Swallow Press, 1954).
4. Ludwig Wittgenstein, *Tractatus Logico-Philosophicus* 5.6 (New York: Routledge, 2001).
5. H. G. Frankfurt, *On Bullshit* (Princeton, NJ: Princeton University Press, 2005).

CHAPTER 3

1. Knute Rockne, "Knute Rockne's Recreation of a Pep Speech," University of Notre Dame Archives, http://archives.nd.edu/rockne/speech2.html.
2. George Bush, "President Delivers 'State of the Union,'" http://www.whitehouse.gov/news/releases/2003/01/20030128-19.html.
3. Cicero *De Oratore,* 2.18.121.
4. Lloyd Bitzer, "The Rhetorical Situation." *Philosophy and Rhetoric* 1 (1968): 1–14.
5. Michael Calvin McGee, "A Materialist's Conception of Rhetoric" in *Explorations in Rhetoric: Studies in Honor of Douglas Ehninger,* ed. Ray E. McKerrow (Glenview, IL: Scott, Foresman, 1982), 23–48.

CHAPTER 4

1. Kenneth Burke, *The Rhetoric of Motives* (Berkeley: University of California Press, 1956), 43.

CHAPTER 5

1. Quintilian *Traditions of Oratory,* IV.1.5.
2. Based on a speech prepared by Danny Horst in 2006 for a public speaking class at the University of Wisconsin–Milwaukee.

CHAPTER 6

1. Aristotle *Rhetoric,* 3.11.9.
2. Richard Nixon, "Eulogy at Memorial Services for Senator Dirksen of Illinois." 1969. http://www.presidency.ucsb.edu/ws/index.php?pid=2229.
3. *Rhetorica Ad Herrenium,* IV.14.21.

CHAPTER 7

1. See Richard Lanham, *The Electronic Word* (Chicago: University of Chicago Press, 1992).
2. George Kennedy, *Aristotle's Rhetoric: A Theory of Civic Discourse* (Oxford University Press, 1990).
3. See Ben Page, *Who Deliberates?* (Chicago: University of Chicago Press, 1996).

INDEX